On the Line:
Women Firefighters Tell Their Stories

By
Linda Frances Willing

JTD Press
PO Box 148, Grand Lake, CO 80447
Linda@rwtraining.com

ISBN 978-1-61043-006-7
Library of Congress Control Number: 2011914674

Dedication

This book is dedicated in memory of my mother
Barbara S. Willing
And for all our mothers who inspire us.

# Table of Contents

# Table of Contents

# Chapter 1

## Women Firefighters
## A Personal Perspective

In 1979, I was 24 and looking for a job. I had spent several years working as a seasonal ranger with the National Park Service at Mount Rainier in Washington State, and then one summer on a trail crew with the Boulder, Colorado Mountain Parks. I loved working outdoors, and hoped to make a career that way, but it was tough. In the 1970s, the park service was inundated with applicants, and even well qualified candidates like me with a college degree and years of experience often had to work seasonally for ten years before finally getting a permanent job. I wasn't sure I could wait that long.

While working for the City of Boulder, I learned about a job with the county parks department that sounded pretty good. It wasn't Mount Rainier, but Boulder parks have wonderful trails, natural features and even spaces resembling wilderness. So I applied for the job and waited, and waited.

In the meantime, my supervisor with the city parks department encouraged me to try to get a permanent job with the City of Boulder. Once I was a full time city employee, I might have preference when applying for other city and county jobs, like the parks job. In the fall of 1979, my trail crew job had run out and I was working with another woman named Eileen, mowing grass and picking up trash in city parks. It was depressing, but it was work.

I started going down to City Hall every Friday to check the job announcements. Everything was done on paper back then, and each job involved multiple pages with the job title, description, specific duties, necessary skills, and required qualifications. I was impatient, as I saw this job search as strictly temporary and expedient. So each week I would look at the first line of the first page where the job title was listed, and if it didn't sound completely disgusting, I skipped to the last line of the last page, where it listed minimum requirements. If I remotely met them, I put in an application for that job on the spot.

In this way, I applied for many jobs, as a groundskeeper and a library assistant and an animal control officer. It is also how I applied for the job as a firefighter. I had no real interest in becoming a firefighter at that time. I wanted to be a park ranger. I really didn't know what firefighters did. Prior to putting in my application, I had never set foot in a fire station.

A few days later, I was at work with Eileen, and as always, the topic of jobs came up. Specifically, we were talking about what we'd rather be doing versus what we were actually doing in that moment, which was picking up candy wrappers that high school kids had dropped in the park on their way back to class. I asked Eileen what she would do if she could have any job.

"I'd like to someday drive the bigger lawnmowers," she told me. I looked at her incredulously. Here was a woman with a college degree in psychology. She was strong and highly intelligent. We had become good friends working together that fall.

I replied, "No Eileen, you don't understand the question. If you could have *any* job, what would it be?"

At this she brightened. "Well, if I could have any job," she said, "I would be a firefighter."

"Really!" I exclaimed. I had never heard of a woman wanting to be a firefighter before. "Why?"

Eileen told me that she was a volunteer with a local fire department, and that she loved fighting fire and driving the trucks. "That's what I would do," she said.

"You're in luck!" I told her. "The City of Boulder is hiring firefighters. You should apply."

"Oh no," she said, her enthusiasm fading. "I applied the last time they hired and I didn't pass the physical test. I'm not going to apply again."

I remember stopping in my tracks and looking at her. "Well, that's just the dumbest thing I've ever heard," I told her. "Look, you already have a permanent job with benefits and a decent salary. It won't hurt you a bit to apply for the firefighter position. If you don't get it, so what? As for me, I don't even want the job. I'll take the test, but I'm really just waiting for that other park job to open up. We can both go take the test, do our best, and then go out for beers afterward. What do you say?"

She agreed. And that's what we did: took the test, went out for beers, and a couple weeks later, Eileen got a phone call that she had been selected. A week after that, I was told I would be hired in the next group, in January 1980.

When I became a firefighter, I had already worked in male dominated, so-called nontraditional jobs for over five years. I had been a backcountry ranger, and been on a trail crew, and worked at a gas station. Firefighting didn't seem like such a stretch, and the more I learned about the job, the more qualified I seemed to be. I was already an EMT for example, and I had some wildland firefighting experience. I had done heavy physical work as a ranger, and was reasonably mechanically oriented. I was a serious rock climber in those days and knew I was strong both physically and mentally.

So I figured I was probably a pretty good candidate, and I also assumed that a lot of women must already be firefighters. Why not? Women had been police officers and park rangers and paramedics for years, why not firefighters? Little did I know.

When I started work as a firefighter in January 1980, there were four other women on the Boulder Fire Department—two who had been hired in 1978, and two who were hired just before me. I was assigned to a shift that had never had a woman on it before. One of the more senior women had also recently been assigned to that shift, but within two months of my hiring, she left the job.

Most of the men I worked with were respectful toward me if not really inclusive. A couple made the effort to be friendly, and a couple others went out of their way to mess with me and set me up for failure. But this was the exception rather than the rule. All in all, things went pretty well for me during my first year on the job.

Of course there were difficulties. Before my personalized bunker gear was made, I wore protective gear left behind by a man who was over six feet tall. I looked like a shar pei dog in that gear, and simply walking was difficult. It was years before I could get a pair of boots that did not require three pairs of socks just to keep them on my feet. For most of my career, my fire gloves were so unwieldy that I had to take them off for every task that required any level of manual dexterity.

One of my coworkers that first year took an interest in my training and made the effort to help me. But when the other guys started teasing him about "liking me," he quit. The main station where I worked did not have any facilities for women other than a closet-sized room containing only a toilet and a sink. By the end of the first year, there were four women working out of that station on different shifts, but we had no lockers, no shower, and no place to change our clothes other than that tiny toilet. I have clear memories of mornings sitting on the steps across from that bathroom, waiting my turn.

But despite the difficulties, I loved the job. I loved going on emergency calls—fighting fire and doing emergency medical work. I enjoyed station life too, the stories and the traditions. The odd schedule suited my lifestyle perfectly. I made a few friends, found a mentor for a brief period of time, and promoted to officer. The job wasn't perfect, but most days it was very good. As a firefighter friend once said, it turned out to be the best uninformed decision I ever made in my life.

One thing that surprised me from the start was the scarcity of women in firefighting. I assumed that there must be many women already doing the job when I became a firefighter in 1980, but I was wrong. At that time, there were probably only around two hundred women in the career fire service nationwide. Many cities did not even consider hiring women as firefighters for another five or ten years.

Toward the end of my first year on the job, my captain came to me with an envelope addressed to the women of the Boulder Fire Department. "This must be for you," he said as he tossed me the letter. It was from a woman firefighter in Ohio named Terry Floren who was doing a survey for a class she was teaching at the Ohio State Fire Academy. I filled out the survey and checked the box indicating that I wanted to be notified of the results.

When Terry followed up months later, I suggested perhaps we could use her small database of women firefighters around the country to create a directory for women to use to find one another. Terry wrote back that she also envisioned starting a newsletter for women firefighters to network with one another and share successes and challenges.

Terry and I became regular correspondents, and by the fall of 1982, we had formed a national nonprofit organization called Women in the Fire Service (WFS). We had our first national conference in 1985 in my hometown of Boulder, and among other remarkable events that week was the fact that it was the first time that Terry and I had ever met in person, after running a national organization together for over three years. For 25 years, WFS put on national conferences, published a monthly newsletter, maintained a website, created publications and videos, represented women's issues on national fire committees, provided expert witness testimony, and provided one-on-one support for women firefighters around the country and the world.

Gradually, over the course of my career, things did change for women in the fire service. More and more women were hired as firefighters, and many promoted to company officer, battalion chief, and even chief of department. The culture of the fire service, always very male, even began to show signs of change, as fire departments started recognizing the need for things like maternity policies and women's locker rooms. Even the deeply ingrained term "fireman" started giving way to the more inclusive (and technically correct) "firefighter."

Fast forward to September 11, 2001. I had left the fire department a few years earlier but was maintaining my ties with the emergency services through consulting and training work, and as an instructor at the National Fire Academy. I was happy with the changes in my life, even as I still always turned my head when I heard sirens in the distance, and frequently dreamed about fighting fire. But that day changed everything.

Never before 9/11 had I felt such a longing to be a firefighter again. The loss of 343 firefighter lives in New York City, the unimaginable horrors witnessed by firefighters at the Pentagon, at the World Trade Center, in Shanksville, Pennsylvania, the community grief that settled over all emergency responders—I wanted to be part of it.

After the initial shock following the attacks on 9/11, I slowly began to notice something strange. Women as emergency responders had disappeared. Oh, they were still out there fighting fires, driving trucks, and leading crews into hazardous conditions. But they were invisible, unacknowledged. In the wake of 9/11, it was all firemen, all the time.

I had been deeply involved with networking among women firefighters for years, and had ties with women in law enforcement and emergency medical services, but it was weeks after 9/11 that I even became aware that women emergency responders had died at the World Trade Center. Two female police officers and one EMT died while rendering aid on 9/11, but I never heard about it until I happened to see a television show over a month later that mentioned the loss as an afterthought. There seemed to be a general assumption among most media sources that no women from the New York City Fire Department had even worked at the World Trade Center on 9/11.

In fact, women were on the scene from the first moments of that terrible day, and continued working at the site for weeks and months after. No women firefighters died on 9/11 (although at least one came very close), but that outcome was a result of statistical probability as much as anything. In 2001, only around twenty women were operational firefighters on the New York City Fire Department, a department of over 10,000 members.

This book is written with the very simple purpose of putting a face on the women who risk their lives as firefighters every day. The women represented here may be paid firefighters on the largest departments in the country, or volunteers on departments with fewer than a dozen people. Some have over thirty years of service, some less than one. They come from a variety of backgrounds; they are a variety of physical and personality types.

One thing draws all of them together: their love for the job of firefighting and their commitment to service for others. None expect special attention, but all appreciate recognition for the work they do and the contribution they make. Here are their stories.

# Chapter 2

## A Short History of Women Firefighters

Although women firefighters are still relatively rare, they have been doing the job for a long time. Most of their history is lost, as women served anonymously alongside the men in their communities, dragging equipment, hoisting buckets, and helping the injured. Only a few names are known from the earliest days.

The first known female firefighter was an African-American woman named Molly Williams, who was held in slavery by a member of the Oceanus Engine Company #11 in New York City. Williams was held in high regard by her coworkers, and particularly distinguished herself fighting fires during the blizzard of 1818. In the 1820s, a French-Indian woman named Marina Betts worked on bucket brigades in the Pittsburgh area. She served as a firefighter for ten years.

In the 1850s, an heiress named Lillie Hitchcock Coit began volunteering with Knickerbocker Engine Company #5 in San Francisco. Until her marriage, Coit was present for every fire with the engine company, which made her an honorary member. For her entire life, Coit wore a gold "5" pinned to her dresses and signed her letters "Lillie H. Coit, 5."

In the late 1800s, women were voted into membership with volunteer fire companies in Atlantic City, New Jersey and West Haven, Connecticut. In Great Britain in 1878, a fire brigade was established at Girton College, an all-women's school near Cambridge. Female students there trained weekly as firefighters under the supervision of a London Fire Brigade captain. The Girton College Fire Brigade existed until 1932 when it was absorbed into the Cambridge Fire Brigade.

In the early 1900s, all women volunteer fire companies were formed in the Los Angeles area to compensate for the shortage of men available to fill these roles. Women trained to operate hand-drawn

hose reels and other fire equipment, and later developed a towing system for the hoses behind their automobiles. At least three different all-women fire companies formed in the Los Angeles area during this time.

Similarly, in Silver Spring, Maryland, an all-women volunteer fire company formed in 1915 and remained in operation for over twelve years. The company boasted that it was "the only fire company manned by women."

The first woman to be officially recognized as a firefighter by the State of New Jersey was Emma Vernell, who became a firefighter at age fifty after her husband died in the line of duty in 1926. Vernell served on the Westside Hose Company #1 (now part of the Red Bank Volunteer Fire Department) for many years.

During World War II, a number of women served as firefighters in the United States and many other countries, to fill in for men who were deployed in the military. Several departments in areas from New York to Illinois were entirely taken over by women during the war. In Great Britain, thousands of women served with the Auxiliary Fire Service (AFS) as dispatchers, couriers, pump operators, and firefighters during the years of the Blitz, when most able-bodied men were away at the front. More than two dozen women active with the AFS died in the line of duty during the war.

The first paid women firefighters in the United States worked as wildland firefighters, starting in 1942 when the California Division of Forestry formed an all-women crew to fight fires in the Soledad area. The crew consisted of a supervisor, a truck driver, an assistant truck driver, firefighters, and a cook. Later, in the early 1970s, the U.S. Forest Service and Bureau of Land Management formed all-women crews in Alaska and Montana. The exemplary service of these crews broke the barriers for women as wildland firefighters, and by the mid-1970s, mixed crews of men and women were the norm.

Women in the United States were hired as career urban firefighters starting in the mid-1970s, with Sandra Forcier Walden hired by the Winston-Salem, North Carolina Public Safety Department in 1973 and Judith Livers Brewer hired with the Arlington County, Virginia Fire Department in 1974. A number of fire departments were put under consent decree during the 1970s to remedy discrimination in

hiring practices related to both race and gender. But whereas th
1970s saw a significant increase in the numbers of African-Am
men hired, it was slow going for women, and by 1980, fewer than
two hundred women worked as career firefighters across the United
States.

Since the 1980s, women have gained a small but solid foothold as
members of the professional emergency services. According to
figures released by the U.S. Census Bureau in 2009, there are as many
as 9,700 career women firefighters in the United States, and many
more who volunteer in various capacities, as firefighters, medics, and
support personnel. A number of women have risen in the ranks of
their departments to become officers, battalion chiefs, and chiefs of
department.

Still, the numbers are small compared to other professions (the same
Census Bureau report estimated that there are nearly 200,000 women
on active military duty, 111,000 female police officers, and 38,000
employed as pilots.) Many women serve their entire careers as the
only woman in their organization. Some fire departments have yet to
hire their first woman.

Women become firefighters for the same reasons that men do: they
want to serve their communities, they are attracted to challenging
physical work that involves some risk, they enjoy working with others
as members of a team, and they like the nontraditional schedule and
working conditions offered by the fire service. Like men, women are
also drawn to the variety of ways that firefighters may ultimately
serve: as line firefighters and officers, as drivers and equipment
operators, as EMTs and paramedics, as special rescue and hazardous
materials technicians, as inspectors and investigators, as community
educators and plan developers—the list goes on and on.

The experience of women firefighters has been as varied as the
people who do the job. Some women are welcomed into their
departments with open arms, and find a sense of community among
their coworkers almost immediately. Others, especially those who

were among the first hired in their organizations, may have had a tougher road to follow. These women not only had to face the challenges of the job itself, but also had to battle exclusion and hostility from coworkers and organizational leaders.

One thing is true for women firefighters the same as men—they do the job because they love it. A common refrain from all women included in this book was that they could not imagine having done anything else in their lives, and that in some ways they felt they were born to be firefighters. The women in this book are part of a proud tradition that goes back hundreds of years, and they carry that tradition forward each day they serve.

# Chapter 3

## Arriving

Showing up is not the same as arriving.

All firefighters are nervous when they first show up for work on shift. Usually they will have gone through recruit school for weeks or months prior to the first day on the line, and that is a time of building skills and confidence. But training academies are also controlled environments where instructors design exercises to be challenging but safe, and lessons learned are planned in advance. All people in recruit school are new and worried about proving themselves; they're all in the same boat.

Things change when as a new firefighter you finally show up at your first station assignment. There is so much to take in—learning the names and roles of other crew members, becoming familiar with the station and assigned apparatus, understanding what is expected of you in terms of station duties, deciphering the unique culture of the station and crew you are assigned to.

All new firefighters want to be accepted among the crews they work with. Such acceptance is a matter of safety as much as social comfort. As one officer said to me early on, "If you find yourself alone, start worrying." He wasn't just talking about the dangers of getting separated from your crew during a fire. He was letting me know about the importance of team, and the fact that no firefighter can ever be successful without the support of his or her crew.

So firefighters show up that first day, nervous as cats and trying not to show it, trying to take it all in and at the same time praying for that critical first emergency call to break the ice.

My first day on the line was an unseasonably warm day in January. I have little recollection of the first few hours of that shift, as I felt both excited and overwhelmed to really be a firefighter. I nearly jumped out of my skin all morning as I heard tones go off for other stations around the city, but not for us. I finally began to calm down at lunch, and I remember the meal was hamburgers with very salty French fries and enormous glasses of ice water to wash it all down.

Lunch was over, and the guys had pushed back their chairs to have a cigarette (times have changed since 1980!) I was feeling a growing urgency to urinate after drinking so much water, but tried to suppress it, as I did not want to single myself out from others by being the first to get up from the table. Finally I could not stand it anymore, and was on my way up the stairs to the bathroom when the call came in for us.

A man down, a few blocks from the station. I did not understand at the time what that meant. I certainly did not expect to roll up on my very first emergency call and find a dead man in the middle of the street.

I had been CPR certified for years, and had finished EMT certification nearly a year earlier. But I had never seen a dead person up close other than in a funeral home, and had certainly never touched one. I don't think it registered for me that this man was dead even as I saw bystanders doing CPR on him.

The feeling I remember when I first arrived at that scene was one of curiosity and surprise more than anything. I felt somewhat detached, even as I recognized the situation as one that was critical. It was my first call on my first day on the job. Certainly no one expected me to do more than observe and provide support.

Then my officer told me take over compressions on the man lying in the street.

My CPR experiences had strictly been on Resusci-Annie, the mannequin used in class. I did not know that those mannequins were stiff and unyielding compared to real people. So I began compressions with the same intensity necessary to pass the CPR class, and immediately felt the man's ribs cave in under my hands.

It was a horrible feeling, but I had to keep going, and continued compressions all the way to the hospital in the back of the ambulance. The adrenaline coursing through my veins made me completely forget about my own physical needs, until I was at the hospital and the resuscitation efforts had been called off. Then I seriously started thinking about finding a bathroom.

I was standing in the emergency room, wondering if it was a good idea to use a restroom in a place full of so many sick people, when my crew appeared at the ER door and motioned to me to come immediately. We had another call.

This time we responded to a car fire. I scrambled into my oversized bunker gear en route to the alarm. When we arrived, we found the engine compartment of a small car completely in flames. I pulled the hose and doused the fire with water from our engine tank while the others disconnected the battery and took down information. They seemed to be taking a very long time to get the information they needed, or maybe it just felt that way as my need to urinate had returned with a vengeance, and being near flowing water was not helping one bit.

I gritted my teeth, and after what seemed like an eternity, we all got back on the engine and headed to the station. But then, a few blocks from salvation (from my point of view), the driver suddenly made a turn and we were off again, with lights flashing and sirens blaring.

This time it was a fire alarm at a preschool. By the time we got there, it had been determined that it was a false alarm, and the offending child had been brought into the office to get the obligatory lecture from the fire officer. At that point I realized I could sneak off, and certainly in a school I would be able to find a bathroom.

I did find a bathroom, but when I entered it, I realized that in my bulky gear there was no way I would be able to fit into a toilet stall designed for a three year old. I just stood there staring and then I laughed. Okay, I thought. Maybe uremic poisoning is just part of the job. I got back on the engine, rode slowly back to quarters, casually got off the rig and stowed my gear, and then nonchalantly went to the bathroom—vowing as I walked in that from now on I would go early, go often, and never turn down an opportunity. That turned out to be a good lesson for the rest of my career.

That night as I lay awake in the dorm listening to the sleep sounds of my coworkers, I relived the rush of the back-to-back calls, and felt the grating of the man's bones under my hands. The feeling gave me chills, but I also felt good, as if I had passed some sort of test.

Arriving as a firefighter is not something that happens all at once. My first day was a good introduction to the job but there were many other events in my career that added to my sense of really being a firefighter. There was the first structure fire, and the first fire fatality. The first auto extrication. The first CPR save. The first death of a child.

And then there were more personal milestones. The first time I stood up for myself, and the first time someone stood up for me. Driving the truck for the first time on an emergency run. My first promotion. The first time I felt truly accepted by my crew and welcomed among them. I remember that day explicitly, realizing how much fun I was having even as we worked hard, and thinking, *now* I understand why people love this job so much.

The sense of arrival as a firefighter is personal and can be expressed by the smallest action—a pat on the back, a positive comment made in an offhand way, an inclusive joke or nickname. These turning points might occur while facing the biggest emergency of your career, or keeping it together when dealing with a small tragedy. Arriving means celebrating success with your coworkers and sharing loss. For the many who have had the sad experience of losing a coworker in the line of duty, arriving means standing shoulder-to-shoulder with other firefighters, united in a sense of service and respect, and being accepted as just another firefighter who is part of the team.

Dee Wooley

Dee Wooley at trench rescue training

## Christmas Shopping

Dee Wooley has been a firefighter for over twenty years, initially with Montgomery County, Kentucky; and since 2001, with the City of Frankfort, Kentucky. Before becoming a firefighter, Dee worked in emergency medical service (EMS). Dee has promoted to sergeant, which on her department is the person who drives the trucks and operates equipment. In 2011, she was assigned as the driver of a 75 foot aerial apparatus.

Dee remembered a turning point for her on the job, her first big fire. "One time when I first came on the job, we had a structure fire and it was one of those early 1900s houses with the balloon construction.

The fire was in the walls, everywhere. When we got there, the other firefighters said, come on sis. I thought, hey they called me sis, that's pretty cool. They even stood aside and let me have the nozzle. That was really something, because you know, everyone fights for the nozzle. They said, go ahead, get in there, show us what you're made of."

"I was fighting fire; it was the first time I had really fought that kind of fire. I came out and said, oh my gosh, oh my gosh. My eyes were the size of saucers. I got to go in, fight fire, be on the nozzle. When I came out, they said, so what did you think? I said, you know, it's bad that people lose their property, but it was, oh my God, a feeling you could not explain."

"When we got back to the station, I was putting my gear in my bag and they said, what are you doing? I said, well the shift's over, I'm going home. And they said, oh no no no, we're taking you out to breakfast. Those guys were awesome. That's when I knew I could do it, and also when I switched over in my career to go over to the fire side of it."

"That was their ritual for the guys, to take you out to breakfast after your first big fire. There weren't any women on the fire department. I came on, not knowing what to expect. And it was new for the guys too, because they had never worked with women before, other than the secretaries. So for them to do that, it meant a lot."

Being accepted as part of the crew meant being included in some off-duty traditions as well. "Every year, the guys would go Christmas shopping. What they'd really do was go to Hooters Restaurant and have wings and watch TV all day, but that was what they'd tell their wives, that they were going Christmas shopping."

"Their wives knew they weren't going Christmas shopping, but the guys would go out and buy some little thing at Walmart and take it back and say, I have to hide this because it's your Christmas present.

They would always invite me to go do that with them. They said, you're one of us, you have to go Christmas shopping with us."

"I want to do the job, do it well, have compassion, and take care of people. When we get on the fire truck and take off, I feel like I'm living the dream. So many people try to get on the job, and I feel privileged to be able to do it." When asked if Dee considers herself a role model, she hesitated, not wanting to appear boastful. But she admits, "I like going to schools and career days to show girls you can go beyond the boundaries of just being a housewife or a secretary. Look what I'm doing. If I can do it, you can do it."

Katja Lancing

Katja Lancing and her daughter Madison at the annual Race for Grace

# First Fire at the Pentagon, 9/11/01

Katja Lancing was working at a hardware store when she first met firefighters and considered a career move to the emergency services. She had recently graduated from college with a degree in psychology and had done an internship at the Pentagon during her senior year. In 2001, Katja became a firefighter with the Fairfax County, Virginia Fire Department, graduating from recruit academy in August. A month later, she got her first fire. It was September 11, 2001.

"I was at Fire Station 30, just a month out of recruit school. Everybody was doing their normal morning chores around the station. One of the guys got on the loudspeaker and said there's a fire in New York. And everybody reacted with, okay, there's a fire someplace every day. No big deal. Then the captain got on the intercom and called us all into the office. We were all sitting there watching what was happening, and another guy and I said, you know, we're surprised they haven't hit the Pentagon, because it's such a landmark in the Washington DC area. And the next thing we knew, the Pentagon was hit."

"We were all watching TV, stunned and amazed by what was happening. Then the phone started ringing, with people from all the other shifts calling in to see if they needed to come in. The department started up-staffing the units as much as they could. Then our tones went off, and we were dispatched to go to the Pentagon. The captain said, grab whatever you need—clothes, food—we're going to be there for awhile."

"At that point my heart dropped. I was scared to death because I was only a month out of recruit school and really didn't know what to expect. We jumped on the engine and headed out to Arlington, where we staged for around five hours in one of their stations, responding to their other calls. At six that night we went to the Pentagon, and we were there until three in the morning. Our main purpose was to search for people in the building and extinguish spot fires. For me, being there really hit home, because it could have been me in that building just a year earlier."

"The impact was adjacent to where I had worked. It was surreal that I had once worked right there. It was very scary and sad, overwhelming really. It could have been me, but now I was on the opposite end of things, helping people instead of needing help."

"We were assigned by the Command Post to enter the building with a hose line and look for victims and fires. We were wearing our self contained breathing apparatus (SCBA) and picking our way through the rubble. It was dark. The roof of the building was gone. Smoke was lingering in the air around us. If we saw anything smoldering or in flames, we put it out. And we were also looking for people. But we didn't find anyone. Just a foot. That was it. No other body parts or any signs of a person. Just a foot."

After Katja's crew was relieved from the scene at three in the morning, they went through decontamination. "They sent us to a firehouse that was designated for decon. We went into a door and they had the entire place blacked out with plastic trash bags. We had to hose ourselves down head to toe with our regular clothes on. We had already taken off our firefighting gear. After we hosed ourselves down, we had to take everything off and put it into a bag—all your clothes, your jewelry, your hair ties, everything. And then we had to go upstairs and take a shower and scrub with this harsh soap, and they gave us clothes, and talked to us a little bit, and then they let us go home."

"It was so strange being naked in some strange fire station, running up the stairs like that, and not knowing where to go. I was sopping wet, it was the middle of the night, and it was not fun. They gave us shorts and tee shirts and little flip flops, and that was all." Katja was the only woman on her crew that night, so they let her go through the decontamination process first. Once she had completed it, the men went through it.

"I feel good about what we did that night. What we did was a small part of what was happening, but the fact we were able to go and serve the people in need, it was a good feeling. The fact that I used to work there made me feel like I was giving back. At the same time, it was also scary because it was such a horrible thing that happened. But I had good leadership that day, and I think that made all the difference. I had confidence in my officer, and being straight out of recruit school, that helped put me at ease."

"I'm proud of being a woman in the fire department. There aren't many of us, and it takes a lot to do the job. I don't think people realize how hard the job really is when you actually have a fire, and what you have to put into it. It's a very satisfying job."

"Since I've been a firefighter, I feel I am a better person, more compassionate. I like to help people more, because of the nature of the job and the ability you have to help people. I've tried to teach that with my children. If someone needs help, try to help them as much as you can. I want to leave that as a legacy with my children."

Michele Fitzsimmons

Michele Fitzsimmons in her FDNY firehouse

# First Fire: 9/11 in New York City

It was only natural that Michele Fitzsimmons should become a New York City firefighter. Her grandfather was a battalion chief with the department, and her great-grandfather was a firefighter who responded to the famous Triangle Shirtwaist Factory fire of 1911. Her father had also wanted to become a New York City firefighter, but was unable to qualify because of a medical issue. "It took him ten years to get over the fact that he couldn't be a firefighter," Michele commented. Since Michele was hired in 2001, her sister has also followed in the family tradition, joining the FDNY in 2006. Michele became a lieutenant in 2007.

Before becoming a firefighter, Michele worked as a program coordinator and advocate for an HIV/AIDS program in New York City. "I was completely burned out from my job. It was very stressful work. I wanted a more hands-on job. I hated having a job where I would come in to a desk and have paperwork to do. I needed something tangible. Just go out and do stuff and have it be done." Michele looked into becoming a police officer, but also considered the fire department. Her battalion chief grandfather did not encourage her. "Women shouldn't be firefighters, he told me. He was very old school."

Michele graduated from the recruit academy in July 2001. Her first big fire came less than two months later, on September 11, 2001. "I was off duty that day. I heard on the radio what had happened, so I turned on the TV and saw it. Immediately there were phone calls. My mother called and asked, what are they going to do? How will they put it out? I had been out of the academy for nine weeks, so I told her what I knew, that they'd hook up to the standpipe in the building, which is standard high-rise procedure. But looking at that volume of fire, I thought, how the hell are they going to do that? While I was talking to my mom, I saw the second plane hit. I told her, I have to go now, Mom. I have to go to work."

It took a long time for Michele to get to her firehouse in Coney Island. Fire department personnel commandeered buses and picked up firefighters from other locations before driving them into Manhattan. When she arrived at the scene, Michele felt, "I can't believe I am here and doing this. I felt amazingly calm in a surreal way. It was such an unprecedented situation. They were just trying to figure out what to do. But I remember feeling that day, I'm really a New York City firefighter!"

"When we arrived there, and the buildings were down, we knew people were dead inside. I knew there was a chance I would know people who were killed." Towers 1 and 2 had collapsed prior to Michele's arrival at the World Trade Center, and Tower 7, a 47 story building at the site, collapsed later in the day when she was there. "I

remember looking at the building and asking the officer, is that
building supposed to be curved like that? We thought maybe it was
an optical illusion at first. But then a little while later, they said, that
building's coming down. So we went to a place of refuge inside the
Woolworth Building, and as we were sitting in there, all of a sudden
we heard it coming down, and then we just saw the blackness across
the windows. And everything went completely dark. Then a little
while later, it slowly started to get gray and then lighten up a little bit."

"We were over on the east side, where the Millennium Hotel was.
Crews were doing fire patrol, checking surrounding buildings. We
were looking for sources of water, because none of the hydrants
worked. They were stretching hose lines from the fire boats and from
many blocks north, trying to get water." When Michele's crew finally
made it over to the west side, where Towers 1 and 2 had been, "that
was when the real scope of it hit. We saw the crushed fire trucks, the
burned out cars. I can't even completely remember now the actual
scale of it that day. Nothing could capture how big it was. We were
like ants on a hill. That's how big it was."

The experience was so intense that ten years later, Michele admits to
having little specific memory of it. "We went over to the west side
around eleven that night and were back in the firehouse by two in the
morning. When I got back to the firehouse, they said okay, you're
back on duty in six hours. Just grab a bunk. But I needed to go home.
So I drove back to my place, but was back at work by eight."

"A lot of overwhelming stuff happened that day. Six guys from my
probie class died that day, including the person who was closest to
me in probie school. But I was really glad I was there and could
maybe do something. I wasn't feeling like I wanted to be anywhere
else. That was exactly where I wanted to be. As crazy as it was, this is
what I signed up for."

"When we first got there, we still had hope we could make rescues.
But I do remember when we saw those collapsed buildings having
this feeling of, I don't know if we'll be able to pull anyone out of

there. It was so huge. How could we possibly get through that? Then days later when we were at the site, it was just so unbelievable that they had been office buildings. Because there was nothing identifiable. Just bits and pieces of things, like a piece of a telephone, the number pad or a receiver. I found a big stack of slides in sleeves, and I remember thinking, how did this survive, but there's not a desk anywhere? It was just pieces—of glass, concrete, steel."

"This is the best job in the world and I wouldn't want to do anything else. I found exactly what I was cut out for. There have been challenging moments, and there have been challenges related to being a woman on the job. But nothing major, nothing that made me feel like, oh my God, I want to quit this job—just, oh my God, today I'm working with a bunch of idiots. I had someone mistake me for someone's eighteen year old son once. My hair was cut short, and I was skinny, and kind of looked like a little boy. A guy came in and said, Whose kid are you? And I said, Huh? I'm a woman! I'm 32 years old! Are you kidding me?"

"I just hope in the long run I am the best firefighter I can be. Maybe I can change a couple guys' minds. It would be great to get more women on the job, considering the fire service as a career option." To aid in meeting this goal, Michele was instrumental in starting the Phoenix Fire Camps in New York, a weeklong program that allows young women to get training and hands-on experience in the fire service. "I hope when I retire, people will say, she was a good firefighter. That would be a great thing."

Michele's grandfather lived long enough to see her become a firefighter. "I had been on the job for a year when my grandfather died. While I was in the fire academy, he came out to see me go through all the training scenarios there. That was a really proud moment for him. At one point he said to me, I guess it's not just a brotherhood anymore."

Brita Horn

# Starting a Fire Department after 9/11

Brita Horn lives in ranch country—244 square miles in northern Colorado inhabited by only 300 people. Her husband's family has ranched the land for generations, and she was content with her life as a wife, mother, and rancher. Then there was 9/11.

"On 9/11, everyone was affected and changed. And this community was too. We are thirty to forty minutes from anybody responding for emergencies here. Literally in the middle of nowhere. So on 10/11 in 2001, a group of us got together and said, we have to make a change. We have to make a difference. And we need to be here for each other and get some local response." That was the beginning of the Rock Creek Volunteer Fire Department, where Brita is currently chief.

By 2002, the department was up and running. It's a very small operation of eight members, with two more preparing to join. The members are all local people who have other occupations— accountants, teachers, ranchers. The department has been built on creativity and generosity. "Everything has been donated to us. We've already had four trucks donated. We've also been fortunate to get grants, six out of the eight I've written."

Brita pointed out that when other nearby departments get grants, her department also benefits. "They give us their hand-me-downs, trucks with fairly low mileage and other equipment. Everyone benefits." When Brita attended a class at the National Fire Academy, her class decided to make its traditional class donation to her department. "I came home with a plaque, $500 in cash, and all these connections. Now we get equipment from all over the country: helmets and PASS devices, and wildland pants, and rubber boots. And they call and say, what else do you need?"

One of Brita's most memorable medical responses came soon after the department was formed in 2002. "It was right after we started, and had been through the fall and winter of training. It was spring then, May 30, 2002. There was a teenager coming back from high school graduation. She was coming up the River Road in a big Chevy pickup and she must have taken a turn too hard, because she flipped the truck. She wasn't wearing her seatbelt and she was ejected about seventy feet, landing on her head. I went with two other men from the community with our ambulance, which was a non-transport vehicle. And the guys said, we can't handle this call, it's your call."

"It was tough, seeing that girl in the middle of the road, her head crushed. She was trying to get up and trying to breathe. She was choking when we were putting her on the backboard. There were so many community members around because everyone was coming home from graduation. It was a big day up here. People were saying, don't touch her, but we told them, no, we're trained, and so we put her on the backboard and tried to keep her airway open. Nobody really knew us as firefighters because we were such a new small group of people, and this was the first big response that we'd had. We couldn't have been more in the center of the bullseye."

"It took forever for the ambulance to come. The firefighters from other departments finally found us. One of them tapped me on the shoulder and said, Where are we landing the helicopter? And I thought, really? You're asking me? I had to help one guy get his GPS to work so the helicopter could find us." Brita and the others helped to load the girl into the ambulance and then the helicopter, but despite everyone's best efforts, she did not survive.

"It was a career event for me, and it was my third call as a firefighter. I was a first responder with this little tackle box that had band-aids in it. We felt we didn't have the tools, we couldn't put her back together. Later a doctor told me if he had everything from the emergency room, he wouldn't have been able to help her either."

"I remember having gloves on during this call, the blue medical gloves, because we knew from our training we were supposed to wear them. But I kept getting blood on them so I put more gloves on over my gloves. I remember pulling them off at the end and someone said, how come you have so many pairs of gloves on? And I said, I don't remember. We had never worked with real blood before. I kept thinking my gloves had to be blue. I don't remember putting the extra gloves on. We were so focused on trying to help her, an eighteen year old girl calling for her mother."

"It was that day when I realized this was my path. There was an ambulance supervisor there and he said to me: Okay, who are you? And when are you going to start in my EMT class? Then the fire department in Gypsum asked me to join." Brita now works in Gypsum as a paid driver/engineer.

Brita's hope for the future is that the department she helped to create is sustainable. "I want us to be successful up here. People know we're up here now, and so many have given so much to help us succeed. In return, I want us to be self-sustaining and have some income, so I don't have to go begging for money every year." Brita's goal now is to create a tax district to support the department. She laughed. "Now we have politicians to deal with."

Sandy Schiess

# The Circle Opens

Sandy Schiess was a recent college graduate when she became a firefighter with the Columbia, Missouri Fire Department in 1978. She was wanting a break from academics, and applied to both the police and fire departments in Columbia, but was ineligible to be a police officer because at age twenty she was too young to legally carry a gun.

The fire department hired her instead, but as she said, "I was pretty naïve about what I was getting into. It was quite a learning curve for both me and the men I worked with. My whole world changed the day I realized that the men were having more trouble with this than I was. In time, we came to the point where we worked together to make the change work for both of us. Once we started looking for common ground, it sure got a lot easier." Today, Sandy works to find that common ground as Chief of the Independence, Missouri Fire Department, an organization of 174 employees serving a community of 122,000.

Sandy remembered a fire early in her career that changed everything for her. "I had been in the fire service for a couple years. I put in for a permanent assignment at a station where the lieutenant said I would be welcome. Little did I know that he had not asked anyone else at the two company station how they felt about me coming there. For the first month, nobody would eat with me. If I came into a room and they were watching TV, they would all leave. They made a point of only opening a driver's position when I was off, so I never got the chance to train on driving. The isolation was really getting to me and I had thoughts of leaving the job."

"One winter morning around 2 a.m., we got a call for a house fire, fully involved. Fire was coming out the windows. I went in as search and rescue after the initial fire attack line. I knew the house because it was right behind my aunt's house, and I knew the people who lived there. In particular, I knew the teenaged boy who lived there, who was a friend of my cousin, and who I'd seen several times over at my aunt's house. My team found him lying beside his bed in the back bedroom. He was fifteen years old."

"We pulled him out and I initiated CPR on him. It was my first fire fatality, and as I did CPR on him, my hands slid on his chest, because his skin was burned and coming off under my hands. Back in those days, we were still doing mouth-to-mouth resuscitation, and when I breathed into his mouth, his skin came off on my lips. I didn't realize it at the time. I was clearing my mouth and wiping my lips, and I was wiping his skin off my face. I looked over and I saw a body covered with a blanket. That was the father. The mother was found dead in her bed. We transported the son to the hospital, but they declared him dead almost immediately upon arrival."

"I had gone to the hospital with the ambulance, doing CPR. By the time I left the hospital, my crew had arrived to pick me up. This was the crew that had never spoken to me or made me welcome in the station. They were standing off to the side, in a circle with their backs to me. I wondered, what the hell am I doing? Then suddenly they looked over at me, and they opened that circle up, and they allowed me to step into that circle. They put their arms around me and we mourned that young man and that family, and we were at that point a team."

"I realized in that moment how important inclusion was, for everyone. It became important to me that no one ever feels as isolated and alone as I had felt. The other thing that changed for me that night was my commitment to fire prevention. This was one of those stories where everything went wrong for that family. The father had fallen asleep while smoking on the couch. When he woke up, the sofa was on fire. There were no smoke detectors in the home. Instead of getting his family out of the house, or calling 911, he tried to get a fire extinguisher to put out the fire. Of course by then, the fire was too big for that to work. And three people died. For me that night, what had started as a fun career full of adrenaline became a mission, to keep people safe, and prevent tragedies like what happened to that family."

A few years ago Sandy was asked to speak at a military base as part of a presentation for women's history month. "I put on my dress uniform and expected to see maybe twenty or thirty people there. But when I arrived, the room was packed, with hundreds of people. And I realized, they were all there to listen to me. I was shocked. They read my biography and I got a standing ovation, and I felt humbled and overwhelmed."

"But then when I stood up to speak, it dawned on me. I said, 'I just realized something. This is women's history month and I've been in the fire service for nearly thirty years, and you've asked me to speak today because you think I'm history!' The thought that you've made history, that you *are* history, is both humbling and hysterical. I was too busy living it to think what it would mean to anyone else. I never looked at it as making history. I just looked at it as making a difference."

# Chapter 4

## Fire: The Reason for Being

Firefighters fight fire. They do a lot of other things too—provide emergency medical care, and rescue people involved in car accidents, and respond to hazardous materials spills, and inspect buildings, and teach children about fire safety, and do housework, and wash the trucks, to name just a few tasks that are part of an average firefighter's day. In fact, fighting fire is only a small part of what every firefighter does, in terms of how time is spent.

But fighting fires is the one thing that only firefighters do, the one aspect of their service that cannot possibly be replicated by anyone else. The equipment required to effectively and safely extinguish fires is expensive and specialized, and maintaining skills requires constant training and practice. Firefighters might go ten years before facing a certain kind of fire, but on that day, they must be able to respond as if they faced that particular challenge every day.

Fighting fire is very hard work and it's dangerous, but most firefighters will admit it is also fun. You really can't be a firefighter without finding some enjoyment in battling flames. Without that adrenaline rush, the job is just dirty, exhausting, and scary.

It's not that firefighters are happy that others have lost their homes or possessions to fire. Far from it. No one knows better than a firefighter how devastating and complete the losses are from fire. It's just that moment, when you see the flames and open the nozzle on them, and you literally feel the weight of the water and steam smothering the fire like a leaden cloud settling over you—well, there's really nothing else like it in the world.

But it's not like most people think. In the movies, the brave fireman (and they're pretty much always men in the movies) runs into the building with an axe and a flashlight, ready to sling the unconscious person over his shoulder so he can carry him to safety. Smoke swirls around like mist in the movies, and firefighters only sometimes wear air packs.

In reality, fire is dark, so dark that you cannot see your hand in front of your face even when it is pressed up against your mask. Fire is also very hot, and heat and smoke rise, so the only place a firefighter can hope to work is in the first two feet above floor level. Get much above that in a really hot fire, and your gear will start to melt.

Nobody runs into a burning building. Firefighters slither into fires like snakes, crawling low, feeling their way along and literally holding onto their coworkers by grabbing a coat or a pant leg, because if you lose that physical contact, you can feel completely lost, even though the other person might be only inches away. Never let go, not of the person or the hose line. They are your lifeline.

Women firefighters, especially those of smaller stature, are often challenged with the question, "Would you be able to carry me out of a burning building?" The implication is that you should be able to throw a two hundred pound man over your shoulder and run out of the building. But this would rarely if ever really happen. You're working at floor level, so real fire rescues involve crawling with victims, not running with them. The equipment is heavy and awkward, no matter who's carrying it.

Firefighting is a team effort; it cannot be done alone. It takes a minimum of two people to advance a hose line, and the more the better. Someone must remain with the engine to pump to the line and monitor water supply. At least two people will be assigned to ventilation, to remove the dense smoke and toxic gases. Someone has to be in command. And then for larger incidents, there are myriad other roles such as emergency medical service and Rapid Intervention Teams, search and rescue and firefighter rehab. The film image of a single firefighter running into the building to save the victim and put out the fire—it never happens.

Fighting fire is some of the hardest physical work a person is likely to do. Firefighters wear bulky protective gear and airpacks that can weigh up to fifty pounds. They carry tools and ladders that add to the burden. They advance hose lines that weigh hundreds of pounds and that are stiff and unyielding. Under these conditions, they work for hours, ascending multiple flights of stairs, or climbing ladders to work on a steep roof, or crawling through basement windows. Wildland firefighters wear lighter gear, but may spend days or weeks on the fireline, digging fire breaks by hand with shovels and Pulaskis, and working up to sixteen hours a day.

You have to love it to keep doing it, year after year, to still feel that jolt of excitement when the alarm comes in for "flames visible." As an officer sitting in the right seat, there is nothing more thrilling and humbling than being first due on a working fire, and knowing it is your job to bring order to the chaos. There is always a moment when you first arrive when you feel small and powerless in the face of the massive energy and destruction of the fire. But then you start to move together as a unit, no longer just one person against it, but the force of a team that will stop at nothing to put the fire out.

For days after the fire, you blow your nose and it's black and sooty, no matter how meticulous you were in using your protective gear.

Even after multiple showers, you will sweat and smell smoke coming from your pores. Fire: it literally gets under your skin.

Komako Goolsby

Komako L. Goolsby with her father, Lt. Kevin E. Goolsby

# First Fire Fatality

Komako Goolsby has been a firefighter/paramedic for the Toledo, Ohio Fire Department since 2006, but she has a much longer history with the fire service than that. Her father, Kevin E. Goolsby, is a lieutenant and thirty year veteran with the same department. "When we traveled as a family, we would always visit a fire station no matter what city we went to. No matter where you go, you always have someone that you know, and you know them because you are a firefighter. They welcome you in." Her father, she said, made the job seem "glorified. And it was something I wanted to be part of."

A former surgical assistant, Komako is a single parent who appreciates how the fire department schedule allows her time to participate more fully in her children's lives. She is also an athlete who regularly competes in the World Police and Fire Games, primarily in track and field events.

Komako remembered a fire early in her career that changed how she saw herself in the job. "There was a fire we went on in the middle of the night, when I had around two years on the job. I was with a fellow classmate of mine who I'd been hired with, and we were both on the back of the engine. The other crew responding to the fire had been stopped by a train, so it seemed like forever for us to get help."

"The other firefighter and I got ready to go into this fire together. It was a brick home, and the fire was rolling pretty good inside. There were neighbors outside saying that someone might be in there. Sometimes when bystanders say things like that, the person usually isn't there. So the other firefighter and I go in, and I had the line and he was backing me up. I yelled out for someone—Hello? Is there anyone here? Make yourself known! Then I saw the fire in the back of the house. It was the room next to the kitchen."

"My only thought was putting the fire out. I knew we were there by ourselves and it would be awhile before the other crews came to assist us. I had a one track mind, and I wanted to put the fire out. I told my partner I needed more hose to get to the back of the house and he tripped and fell. I turned around and asked him if he was all right. And he had a look on his face, like a deer in the headlights. He said, I think I found the victim. He had actually fallen over her."

"I dropped the line and went to help him. The woman's body looked all right, but from the neck up, she was badly burned. And I felt really bad because she was right by the front door. How could we have missed her? Could I have saved her life if I had not been so hell bent on putting out the fire first? Could I have looked harder or searched better? If only I had squatted down a little bit, or just not been so focused on putting out the fire as a young probie. The chief said no,

41

you couldn't have saved her. But maybe the situation could have turned out differently. This was my first fire death. And it taught me that I need to really see the big picture first, no matter what."

"I try to recruit other women to the job. They have this preconceived notion that it's this scary career where you go into burning buildings and you might die. In actuality, with all the safety procedures we have now, and the better gear, it's not like it used to be. There are so many opportunities. You don't have to be on the engine all the time. I do a lot of public education, filling in to speak at the schools."

"My father and I were the first father/daughter on the department, so we got a lot of media attention. In one interview, they asked me what my goals were, and today they are still the same. I want to be the first black female lieutenant, captain, and chief on the department. I want to set a precedent. I didn't come on this job to just enjoy the benefits. I came on the job to contribute. I want to show everyone I am a full time contributor in any capacity I may be needed, in any way I can help. That's what I want to accomplish."

Anna
Schermerhorn-Collins

Anna Schermerhorn-Collins at Phoenix Fire Camp

# 9/11 in New York City

Anna Schermerhorn-Collins was a graduate student in New York City in the early 1990s when she suddenly became interested in the fire department. At an impasse with school, she took a leave of absence, fairly certain she would not return. Anna lived in Upper Manhattan at the time and frequently saw fire engines on the streets. "I got curious. What did they do? It was something exciting and completely different from what I had grown up around. I got this crazy idea that maybe I wanted to be a firefighter." She applied for the job in 1991 and was finally hired off the list in 1996. In 2005, she promoted to lieutenant.

On September 11, 2001, Anna was off duty and sleeping late. She was awakened by a phone call from her sister-in-law in Texas. "I knew something was wrong for her to be calling then. When I picked up the phone, the first thing she said, was, 'Oh thank God you're there.' Then she told me to turn on the TV." It was shortly after the first plane had hit the World Trade Center. Anna knew immediately that a recall of fire personnel was coming, and that she needed to get to the firehouse as quickly as possible.

At the time, Anna and her fiancé lived in the North Bronx. They did not own a car. As they walked down the hill to the subway, they could see the smoke plume rising over Lower Manhattan. When they arrived at the subway station, a train went by. They did not realize that it had been the last train. All public transportation service had been cut off. "So we walked, at least trying to get into Manhattan and work our way from there." They walked by a man in a pickup truck who was telling a police officer he was a firefighter and needed to get through. "I told him I was a firefighter and needed a ride to wherever he was going."

Anna finally arrived at the firehouse around eleven in the morning, after both towers had collapsed. A group of off-duty firefighters had assembled there. The regular crew and apparatus had responded to the World Trade Center hours earlier. "We were directed to collect equipment—tools, medical supplies, anything we could grab. There was a lumber company across the street and they had a flatbed truck, so we loaded it up. We commandeered a city bus, and were all loaded up, ready to go to the scene when the battalion commander came on the bus and looked at all of us and said, Guys, I hate to tell you this, but we're not going anywhere."

"At that point, we had ideas about the severity, but we really didn't know. You still think people got out. Then I saw two guys who were assigned to Ladder 3, Battalion 6 walk down the street in the mid-afternoon, back toward the firehouse, and they were completely covered in pulverized concrete. I looked into their faces; their eyes were glassy and lost. And that's when I realized this is really, really bad. That's when it dawned on me that a lot of our people had died, people I worked with and people I knew well, very likely all dead."

At one point, Anna's battalion commander came to her and asked her if she had called her parents. "I told him I hadn't. It didn't even occur to me to call them. I was so much in the here and now and what needed to be done. And I had talked to my sister-in-law that morning and she knew I was all right. But that was before everything collapsed. She told me later that she thought she had sent me into it."

Anna finally arrived at the scene around six that evening. "Everything was covered with brownish gray dust. It was beginning to get dark. It was like a volcano had erupted. We wanted to find our crews, Ladder 9 and Engine 33, so we just wandered, looking for them. Nothing was recognizable. You really didn't know where you were unless you saw a street sign."

"Then we got to the corner of West and Vesey, and across from where the North Tower had been we saw Engine 33. It was hooked up to a hydrant and the pump was running but none of the crew was there. It was right across from where the North Tower had been. I thought, how can this be? The engine looked good, hardly damaged. Everything around it was destroyed. It was just the way things fell. So I went into the cab and got the riding list, anything that said who had been on the engine when it responded." Anna later learned that only the Engine 33 driver had survived the collapse. In all, Anna's station lost ten firefighters on 9/11.

Eventually, in subsequent weeks, Anna's battalion got both Engine 33 and Ladder 9 back. "It was nearly a year before these rigs were completely cleaned, inside and out. When we would go to the firehouse in the months that followed, that smell was always there. The smell was in the rigs, the smell was in Lower Manhattan, the smell was anywhere south of 14th Street. The smell was in the firehouse, the smell was in your gear. It was the smell of the destruction, and there were some concerns that the rigs had never been properly decontaminated, and it would make us sick. But you know, it was a funny thing, but I actually feared the day that I wouldn't smell that smell anymore. Because I knew when that happened, it was all gone."

"It was horrible, but in the terrible things that happened, a lot of amazing things also happened. The way that we all worked together afterward was critical, and I'll never forget it. It was a unique time in the fire department, in the year that followed. We bonded in a way that I don't think I'll ever bond with a crew again. We all really needed each other. We had shared an experience that you really didn't want to talk about with other people, but we would talk with each other. We didn't have to explain a lot. The others knew what you were feeling. It was the worst of times but at the same time, it was part of my career that long after I am retired will be defining for me as a firefighter."

Anna spent a month at the World Trade Center site in April, searching the debris. "We really didn't find much. But that's a part of my career I am most proud of, that month of cleanup. It felt like it really mattered to be there. I knew because of the people we lost and their surviving families, that it was really, really important to try to find whatever we could. It was critical that we do that. And I hope we never have to do it again."

"The fire department has been wonderful. It has given me so many opportunities, opened up doors." In 2005, Anna attended a national conference for women firefighters, and she and another FDNY firefighter participated in a workshop on creating summer fire camps for girls. "Michele and I looked at each other and said, we have to do this." They happened to meet a New York State fire official at the same conference, and after a few conversations, Phoenix Fire Camp was born.

"We started planning in spring of 2005, and got it up and running in 2007. By the seat of our pants, we pulled it together and had ten campers that first year." The camps are designed to introduce young women ages 14-19 to the career of firefighting, including a lot of time spent teaching hands-on skills. Anna still keeps in touch with many girls from that first summer and subsequent camps. "Some of them have since gone into fire or emergency services. And for the women who have been involved in teaching at the camps, it's been great. Now I have these friendships with firefighters from all over the state."

"It is so great to keep hearing from these gals who have been through the program and to see where they're going. Some of them are lieutenants in their volunteer fire departments now. Some are EMTs. It's incredible. These girls are like my nieces. We've really made a difference in their lives. That's what I am most proud of."

Debra Addison

# 9/11 at the Pentagon

Debra Addison never considered becoming a firefighter when she was growing up. As one of five sisters in a family with no sons, she thought about becoming a nurse. But then her older sister Diane started volunteering as a firefighter, and in 1979 was hired by the Washington DC Fire Department as one of the first women on the department. "She talked me into it," said Debra. "She took me to classes to prepare me for the test, and in 1980, I took the exam. Three years later I was hired." They were the first sisters to serve on a major metropolitan department. Debra retired as a truck company lieutenant in 2009.

On September 11, 2001, Debra was attending paramedic school. It was only the second day of class. "The ground shook. We didn't know what happened. We didn't know that we had just heard the plane hit. Once we found out what was going on, within thirty minutes we were on our way back to the training academy. We put together crews on the apparatus that was at the academy and we responded to the Pentagon. One minute I was sitting in class, and the next minute I'm going across the bridge to Alexandria to the Pentagon."

"There was no time to think about anything. We could see the black smoke rising from the site. The first thing I heard when we arrived was a chief saying that we might have to take a dive, because they'd just had word another plane was coming. I remember thinking, how did I end up in the middle of a war zone? I signed up for house fires! My family pictures were flashing in front of my face, and I didn't know if I would ever see anyone again. And there I was, right in the middle of it."

Debra's crew arrived at the scene within an hour of the plane striking the building. "The scene was chaotic. There were pieces of the plane laid out on the ground. Cars that were parked next to the building were completely burned out. There were bodies everywhere that the Pentagon personnel were trying to get covered and moved away from the building. We rotated in shifts to go in to fight the fire. There were rooms where people were dead and you couldn't tell who was white and who was black. They were all just charred in their places. I remember seeing shoes all over the place and thinking, people were in these shoes."

The experience at the Pentagon was horrific. "We were out there in that smoke, and it seemed like forever. We knew it was terrorism, and we all thought, did they have something on that plane, some chemical or something that would kill us all?" And then there was the sheer magnitude of the death, suffering, and destruction around them. "It wasn't just inside. Before we got there, some folks were able to get some people out who were burned real bad. People with body parts missing. People who were already dead. Parts of the plane were scattered on the ground. It was so disorganized, with all the different agencies there. It was before we adopted unified command."

"I had never been on such a chaotic scene. Everyone's phones went down, so we couldn't call our families. Nobody in my family knew I was at the Pentagon. They knew I left to go to school. I didn't know if I would ever see them again. No one knew what was going to happen. We were afraid, anxious, but no one fell apart. We all managed to keep it together even though it all seemed so unreal."

"I had seen a lot in my years on the department by that time. But that was just devastating. Some of the people who had been in paramedic school with me and who had responded over there could not do the class anymore. We had to have a psychologist come in and talk to the class. But still some people had to leave."

"I would not trade my years on the fire department for the world. I got to meet some crazy people and some very nice people. When I came on, there were only around a dozen women on the job. A number of fire stations had never had a woman work there. So it was an adjustment period for them, but also for me, because I didn't grow up with brothers. When I would walk into the room sometimes and there were eight or ten of them, and only one of me, and if they were talking about something I really didn't want to hear about, I'd just walk out of the room. I didn't make a big deal out of it. Overall, I got the utmost respect. And after time, they did adjust."

Becoming an officer was a turning point for Debra in her firefighting career. "I didn't turn into a monster because I made officer. But I was serious when I was at work. I always stood up for my crew and treated people fairly. They knew where I stood. Everybody respected that because I didn't treat one person differently from anyone else. And I worked along with them. I wouldn't tell them to do something I wouldn't do. I was really proud of that."

A true sign of success came one morning at shift change. "I had to hold over because neither the truck nor the engine had its regular officer there that day. And the two drivers of the truck and the engine were arguing over whether I would be the officer on their rig. Little things like that made me proud. Because if I'm not doing my job, they're not going to want to work with me."

Cheryl Clark

Cheryl Clark at confined space training

## Putting a Face on Fire Loss

Cheryl Clark has been a firefighter in Ohio since 1988. Initially hired with the town of Fairborn, Cher moved to the Dayton Fire Department in 1992, where she is currently a captain. Before becoming a firefighter, Cher was a single mother who worked as the manager of a bar and restaurant.

"The guys from Dayton Fire would come out to the bar after their shifts for what they called 'choir practice.' We weren't normally a place that was open in the mornings, but some of the guys asked if we would. So we opened for them, and served Bloody Marys and breakfast." It was one of those Dayton firefighters who suggested that Cher apply for the job. "I'd never considered the fire service. I was so naïve. I had no idea how competitive it is to get on the fire department. I thought, okay, I'll start reviewing and I'll start working out, and I'll take a test and get hired. I had no clue that people tried for years to get on a department and never made it. Probably it was to my advantage that I was so clueless."

Cher remembered an important lesson learned from a routine fire early in her career. "There wasn't anything about the fire itself that stood out for me. It was what happened afterwards that left an impression. It was a room and contents fire in a ranch house. It was nothing big, but there was a lot of damage to the contents of the house. It was a nice day out, and afterward we were all standing around and cracking jokes like we do after fires. We felt pretty good because we'd gotten in there and put a good stop on the fire."

"We were out there laughing and talking together when down the sidewalk came this pizza guy, wearing a Domino's Pizza uniform. So we started cracking jokes about how we didn't think anyone in this house ordered a pizza, and hopefully you're not delivering there. We all thought it was hilarious. Then we saw him walk up to the incident commander and talk to the chief, and we found out it was his home that had burned. I felt awful. I wished I could have crawled into the sewer."

"The guy was a renter and had no insurance. He had lost a lot of his property. It was really the first time I was aware of the impact on the person whose house it was we were responding to. When I first came on the job, fighting fires just seemed like fun and a challenge. But that day I was faced with the personal loss from the fire."

"Since then I have been more aware of my surroundings and the personal impact the incident has on the people involved. Some of the guys, when they are doing overhaul, will grab drawers of people's belongings and start throwing them out the window. I'll tell them to stop. That day had a huge impact on me. I wasn't proud of myself that day. But I learned something important as a result."

"Being a firefighter has been a constant reminder to be grateful for the things I have. Even just small things, like how grateful I am for a hot shower after a nasty fire. There's nothing like that first shower once you're back in quarters and everything just kind of washes away. I'm grateful for the life that being a firefighter has afforded me. Dayton has a lot of people who are living in poverty. I feel so fortunate not to have been in their shoes."

"I hope people say I'm capable and that I care. That I am compassionate. Some of the guys will talk about certain neighborhoods or the people who live there. But I don't know what kind of life they've had or what has brought them to this apartment or house in this time. It's not my place to judge what may have gone wrong in their lives. It's my place to help them have something better, to help them with whatever their emergency is."

"Sometimes other guys will be making comments, and I'll hear them say, 'Well, we know Cher doesn't agree with us.' Because I have disagreed with them before. And most of the time, they will stop. Initially I was too shy or self-conscious to speak up. But once I did start speaking up, most of the people honored that. And now being a captain, it is part of my job to set the tone. I think it is a lack of leadership if people won't stand up. It all goes back to the people who are in charge."

Amy Brow and crew rehabbing after a fire

Amy Brow

# From Research to Reality

Amy Brow has been a member of the Ann Arbor, Michigan Fire Department since 1992 and is currently a lieutenant. She describes her career as one with some trials and tribulations, "and right now, we're more in the tribulation state." Money is tight and her department has been downsized from 125 members when Amy was hired to only 86 in 2011. "One fire station has already been closed, and they want to close another one." Losing members makes it harder to provide service to the community as well as keeping firefighters safe.

In 2011, Amy was in the process of finishing up her Executive Fire Officer (EFO) certification through the National Fire Academy, the first on her department to complete this prestigious four year program. One of the program requirements is writing thesis-length research papers on topics of relevance to the modern fire service.

Amy remembered how her course work with the EFO program went from academic to very real a few years ago. "I was in my second class with the EFO program, Community Risk Reduction. I had noticed in Ann Arbor that we had had quite a few couch fires on porches in off campus housing." (Ann Arbor is home to the University of Michigan.) "I took that on as my topic and did a paper, and I was just getting ready to send it in. So I was very familiar with the dangers of having a couch on a porch and the fire hazard surrounding that."

"It was Good Friday of 2009. We got called at five in the morning that Friday, and it came in as a porch fire caused by a garbage can. So initially we thought it wouldn't be much. But then they updated us that it was a couch that was on fire. So I told my guys, this is going to be something. Be ready."

"When the first engine arrived at the scene, they had one kid running out from the house completely engulfed in flames. Three more kids were jumping out the back and had to be rescued with ladders. This fire meant something to me because it really drove home the dangers of what I had been writing about. The one student ended up dying from his burns."

"As a result, the city council and the boy's parents managed to get an ordinance passed to ban couches on porches. A similar attempt had been made five years earlier, but had failed. But now they were able to get it passed. It made me feel good that I had picked a topic that really needed to be addressed, although of course so tragic that someone had to die to get people's attention. That fire really hit home. It meant something to me. The research I had done turned out to be exactly what happened that night."

"When I came up on that fire, it seemed like organized chaos, as many fire scenes are. The injured boy was still alive and talking to us then. The driver of the tower ladder had patted the fire out on the boy and got his melting skin on her hands. When you hear somebody's voice, and you hear it a pitch higher than what it normally is, you know the seriousness of the situation. When the captain said, I need ladders back here, I have people jumping, you know, this is it."

"We had a report there was still somebody inside and the stairs were burned through so it was hard to search the building. My crew members knew I had been working on that paper for a long time, and that night they could see it with their own eyes. We videotaped a walk-through of the burned out building after the fire, and plan to use it for training purposes."

"Being part of the Executive Fire Officer program is what I am personally most proud of in my career. The program has made me more responsible in a global sense. I don't just look at a call as a call anymore. I think about how it could be managed differently. The EFO program has given me a better ability to look at the whole picture. It's certainly made me a better lieutenant and I hope someday will also make me a better chief."

Mary Cooper

## The Worcester Fire

When Mary Cooper applied to be a volunteer firefighter with the town of Boxborough, Massachusetts in 1984, the chief asked her if she had checked the wrong box on her application. Certainly she meant to apply to be an EMT and not a firefighter? No, replied Mary, I want to join the fire department. She became the first woman to serve as a firefighter in Boxborough.

Mary served as a firefighter and paramedic until November 20, 2000, when she was critically injured as a result of an 18-wheeler truck hitting her car. When she awoke after more than two weeks in a coma, she was told that she had a spinal injury that would make her a paraplegic for the rest of her life. "At that moment, I lost my job and my career. But even though I cannot work anymore, I still believe that a woman can do anything she wants if she works for it, and I am teaching my daughter these things."

On December 3, 1999, Mary was working an overnight shift for a private ambulance company when she heard a major fire call come in for the Worcester Fire Department, in the next town over. "We sat up all night and listened. We were sitting up on the edge of the beds as things unfolded, and we heard that firefighters were trapped, and they couldn't find them. It was horrible sitting on our hands, knowing we couldn't go."

"The next morning when I got off work, the District 3 Hazardous Materials team that I was part of had been activated." The team had a large communications van that was called to the fire scene to support the operation. By then, six Worcester firefighters were missing and presumed dead at a fire in what turned out to be an abandoned warehouse. At the time, it was one of the worst losses of firefighter lives at a single incident.

Initially, Mary and others worked as support services for the Worcester Fire Department at the scene. "By morning, the entire building had collapsed. Our job was to support the fire department in a kind of tent city that had been set up. We supported the Worcester firefighters as they went into the building to find their fallen comrades. Home Depot had donated wood, sawhorses, heaters, anything we needed. So we would go get the materials and set things up, and we also talked to the families who came to the scene, and kept them warm in the tents. It was December, and very cold."

"Later, Worcester sent out a call saying they needed coverage for their stations, since so many of their people were at the fire scene. Towns from thirty or forty miles away sent trucks and covered for fires in Worcester. I was a senior firefighter in Boxborough so I was one of the people who went to cover at the central station in Worcester. All these old timers came in while we were there. The atmosphere was

for Being

ny night there, and they told me that I was the
'er to ever spend the night in the central firehouse
an honor that they would allow me to do that."

ᴊᴊ Worcester firefighters from being on the hazmat team.
..ᴜ of the older guys hated women on the hazmat team. They were so biased toward them. One of them had been a firefighter forever. So I just made it a point to make him like me. And we did become friends when he realized I was doing the job. It just took him awhile. For me, that was a real sense of acceptance, that the older Worcester guys said I could do it. That made me feel good."

The recovery of bodies at the fire scene took over a week while the fire continued to burn in the collapsed structure. For Mary, the loss was personal as well as professional. "One of the firefighters who was lost was Jerry Lucey, who had been on the hazmat team with me. We had just done a hazmat response together the week before. We were both working support at the scene. I remembered sitting with him on the side of Route 90 goofing off between washing off the firefighters as they came out of the hot zone. He was the nicest guy. And just a week later, he was dead."

Mary remembered standing by while the firefighters' remains were recovered at the scene. "Every time someone came out with some remains of the firefighters, the fire still burning in the walls would come up and you could see it through a lone window. The fire would shoot through the window, every time. Then as soon as the person was brought out, it would become silent again. When the last person came out, it did it one more time, and that was it. It was really weird. It was truly an act of God. You could see the fire through the window, and then it would die down once they were gone. Every time they brought someone out, everyone would line up on both sides and men would just cry."

"I am proud that I was a firefighter. I am proud that I can tell my daughter about all the crazy stuff I did when I was younger. I'm proud that I was able to pave the way for future women firefighters."

Christine Bahr

Christine Bahr in a Life Flight helicopter

# The Oakland Hills Fire

In 1988, Christine Bahr was painting Victorian houses in San Francisco and saving money for graduate school when she first thought about joining the fire service. "I carried 35 foot ladders in my painting job and worked at extreme heights, which were some of the things that made me feel I could be a firefighter." Chris was originally hired as one of the first women on the San Francisco Fire Department, but ultimately made her career with the South County Fire Department until her retirement in 2000.

On October 20, 1991, Chris was at work on what was shaping up to be a normal Sunday in the firehouse. The Forty-Niners were playing

in Candlestick Park that afternoon, and the second
Series was scheduled that evening. Chris was
'one of the TV cameras picked up a wide-angle
?ark and the newscaster commented on the dark
⌐eyond the bay in Oakland." A few minutes later, the
-wscaster confirmed that a fire was burning in the Oakland Hills.

As the fire grew, mutual aid and strike teams were called from around
the area. Chris and her crew were part of the Southern Strike Team,
which was soon mobilized. "As we drove to Station 9 [to assemble
with other team members] I could see dense haze hanging in the east
spreading toward us." Chris noticed two things that seemed very
wrong: "the flags were blowing the wrong way, and the temperature
was way too hot for October."

As her crew drove toward the fire, Chris tried to protect herself from
the scorching heat in the open rear jump seat of the engine. "The
diamond plate that covered the engine next to me was so hot I had to
spread my turnout coat over it to keep from being burned." As they
got closer to the Bay Bridge, Chris saw "black litter flying through the
air like scorched butterflies. I snatched a singed piece of paper
floating over my head. It was a page from a cookbook, which
crumbled in my hand like a dried leaf."

Once in Berkeley where they were instructed to stage, Chris began to
see the real effects of the fire. "The sounds of sirens and air horns
filled the air along with ash and floating embers. People were
standing on the sidewalks holding their hands to their mouths. In the
hills above, I could see flames churning through clouds of smoke,
and along the ridge I could see homes falling to the firestorm."

As her strike team headed into the fire zone, "we drove out of bright
sunlight into strange darkness. On both sides of us we saw flaming
brush and sputtering eucalyptus trees, telephone poles arcing like
Fourth of July sparklers, crazily abandoned cars still burning, dozens
of isolated spot fires along the road lighting our way like medieval
torches. We passed a thirty foot jet of blue flame—a broken gas

line—and heard explosions all around us. It looked like someone dropped a bomb on Oakland."

Chris and her crew arrived in an area where houses were still standing near Broadway Terrace. "I heard the captain of Engine 12 on the radio urging Battalion 3 to make a stand there. He thought he could save those homes." There were five engines, but only 2500 gallons of tank water among them. "What the captain was saying was on all our minds—how can five engines just stand by while houses are on fire? But we also realized that this narrow street was too dangerous a place to make a stand, and that there was really nothing we could do to save those homes. So we moved on."

Ultimately, Chris and her crew set up an operation at the intersection of Broadway Terrace and Hermosa, fighting fire for hours through the evening and into the night. In this effort, they changed from wildland back to structural firefighting gear, and took hose lines into homes. In the first house, "at first things looked okay. The air was clear and we could see around us." But when the four of them went upstairs, "the room was immediately enveloped in smoke and too hot to stand up."

"We punched holes in the ceiling and pulled down the sheetrock trying to extinguish the fire raging in the attic space. I punched through a wall with my axe and saw a lot of fire inside." When another firefighter opened a door in the room, the fire intensified and "smoke was sucked away into the flames. The officer yelled to back out right at the moment that everything in the room reached its ignition temperature"—a flashover.

As Chris and her crew tumbled down the stairs and out of the house, "I saw photographs hanging on the wall at the landing. I snatched them off the wall and wrapped them in a towel I found hanging beside a door." Chris put the saved photos in a neighbor's yard in a place she felt might be safe from the fire. It was the only thing she was able to salvage from any of the homes they tried to save that day.

The backbreaking work continued through the night, with some saves and more losses. "We were essentially fighting the wind. Our training and experience had nothing to do with putting out this fire. We knew everything from Piedmont to the edge of the bay could be incinerated as long as the wind kept up. The only way to stop this fire would be an act of God."

At two in the morning, Chris's crew was able to take a short break. Chris found a place to lie down in the hose bed of the fire engine. "I was curled up on top of a pile of hose, breathing through a filthy bandana, and I looked up at the sky and saw stars shining down on us. The wind had died down. It was a miracle."

By dawn, Chris's part in the Oakland Hills fire was mostly over. Relief crews from all over the state were streaming in by then, and her crew was headed to rehab and then home. "As we crawled out of the scorched and smoking hills toward the neighborhoods that were fortunate enough to be left intact, we began to see signs of life. The streets were lined with people waving and giving us the thumbs up sign. The people on the streets and even the cops directing traffic acknowledged us like heroes, but I didn't feel like a hero. Strangely, now that the work was done, I felt empty and unprepared for what would happen next. My assignment was to go home, but I wasn't sure I even wanted to go. How could I wash this experience off in the shower?"

On October 24th, Chris returned to the neighborhood where her engine had made its stand. The fire was out, but not before consuming over 3000 homes and claiming 25 lives, including an Oakland Fire battalion chief and an Oakland police officer. "I had made index cards with the names of the engine companies who fought to save homes in the area, and I left the cards on doors and in mailboxes." At the same house where Chris's crew had been caught in the flashover, two women appeared from the burned out building. "I told them I was in their home last Sunday night and I wanted them to know what we did. I also asked them if they found their photographs. Yes, they had, the daughter said. Thank you, she said. Thank you so much."

"Then I stopped at Cochrane Avenue. Standing in the driveway to what was once the home of friends, I thought how familiar this scene looked to me: the twisted pipe and warped kitchen appliances, the feathery layers of ash defining an antique dresser, a record collection, a piano, Halloween-like trees guarding nothing. After all, I had seen hundreds of homes just like this. I was staring out at the panoramic view of San Francisco, made more splendid by the absence of a few hundred homes, when my friend walked up and stood beside me. 'Sorry the house is a mess,' he said. I hugged him and I finally cried."

# Chapter 5

## Up Close and Personal:
## Emergency Medical Response

In some ways, providing emergency medical service is the opposite of firefighting. Fires tend to be large in scale—even the routine room-and-contents fire may involve multiple engines, a command post, and support personnel. Most firefighters never meet the people whose homes are damaged or lost since it is not necessary to have that personal contact to get the job done. Fires are an event, a challenge, a battle. Not a relationship.

Emergency medical care is where the job of firefighter truly has a human face. Medical care requires direct contact, a physical touch. This level of personal contact is not just so firefighters can provide the technical means to save lives with procedures and equipment and drugs. Firefighters also provide the critical presence of strength and safety for those whose lives have been disrupted.

Emergency medical work is what most firefighters do most of the time. Some of them are paramedics, trained and skilled to operate nearly autonomously in the field. Others are basic care providers with few resources beyond stopping the bleeding and holding a hand. In either case, firefighters who arrive at the scene of a medical emergency provide critical service, and not just in a medical way.

Some people wonder why firefighters go on medical calls. If someone has a heart attack, why not just send an ambulance? Those people may not understand that firefighters perform many functions on medical calls. All firefighters are trained to provide some form of medical care, but it's more than that. Firefighters control the scene. They safeguard victims in traffic or other hazardous conditions. They remove injured people from vehicles with specialized tools. They aid in extricating people from confined spaces and carrying them down three flights of narrow stairs to the ambulance. In the most critical cases where CPR is being performed, it is usually the firefighters who are doing compressions while paramedics are preparing drugs and establishing airways. Emergency medical care is a team effort.

Firefighters do get impatient and worn out sometimes when responding to trivial medical calls that really do not require their presence. Maybe it's the homeless person who is always drinking too much or the elderly woman who falls out of bed and calls 911. Maybe someone else could provide the needed care without a fire truck being involved.

But there is something to be said for the calming presence of a firefighter. Even the most wrecked fifty year old homeless person probably loved fire trucks when he was five. Elderly people naturally trust firefighters. The care firefighters provide on medical or rescue scenes goes far beyond the technical.

Emergency medical care does involve forming a relationship with the patient, even if only for a few minutes. Trust and effective communication must be established. Family members must be considered. On an emergency medical call, a firefighter has to look into a man's eyes and tell him that his wife of sixty years is gone. It takes a different kind of skill and courage to do that job well.

Every emergency medical call is a short story waiting to be written. Emergency medical response encompasses everything from the most tragic and horrible to the ridiculous or even joyful. There was the woman who called 911 because she was having "an out of body experience" (only in Boulder!) and the man who dropped a running circular saw on his leg, but was mostly worried about not getting blood on the new carpet. The indigent man suffering from alcohol poisoning whose luminous drawings adorned his otherwise squalid apartment. The elderly woman dressed as if for church at five in the morning, waiting to receive the emergency responders on her husband's last day alive. The suicide, the murder, the unexplained death among friends in a movie theater. The first CPR save. The birth of a baby, and the death of another.

As a firefighter, I always felt honored to do emergency medical response. The trust that people gave us, just because of who we were, was astonishing at times. They would answer every question, divulge the darkest secrets, allow us the most intimate physical contact. They gave us unlimited access to their homes, were happy to have us take care of their children, and included us with gratitude as they experienced the worst day of their lives.

Most people will never experience a fire in their lives, but the odds are good that they will be in an accident or need help with the illness or injury of someone close to them. At that point, when they are helpless, afraid, in pain, or grappling with loss, a firefighter is often the first person they will see. For firefighters, there is satisfaction in being able to face such loss and not turn away, but instead to meet the other's gaze and put one's hands out to help, up close and personal.

Denise Allen

Denise Allen ready to respond

# Snowbank Rescue

Denise Allen is a busy woman. Since 1996, she has worked as a per diem (paid per shift) firefighter/paramedic for the towns of Windham, Falmouth, and Cumberland, in rural Maine. In addition, she has been a high school biology teacher at Greely High School for seventeen years. Denise spends the day at school and then often picks up a 6 p.m. to 6 a.m. shift at the fire station that night. She usually adds a 24 hour shift over the weekend. Her two certified therapy dogs accompany her to her day job.

At age 39, Denise is now considering going to medical school. She commented, "One thing I want to say about being driven is that a lot of people say you have no life. But I have a great life. It's my life, it's the life that I choose. It just doesn't look like other people's. I'm not subscribing to society's definition of what a happy life is. Because I'm pretty darn happy."

One rescue call that stuck with Denise happened a few winters ago. "Two teenaged boys had made a fort in a snowbank in a church parking lot. The snow was really deep. The kids had been missing for hours. What people didn't realize was that a plow truck had come through the parking lot and plowed them in. The snow had collapsed on top of them. They had been in that snowbank for at least six hours."

"We followed the tracks from their house to this snowbank and we were digging and digging and calling their cell phones and it really seemed almost like a futile attempt. Would we find these kids alive? I was digging this hole from the top down where we thought they might be in the snowbank and someone was holding onto my bunker pants so I wouldn't fall in on top of them, and I saw this kid's head. I really thought he was dead when I started uncovering his head."

"Then the boy pushed his hand up through the snow and grabbed my hand and wouldn't let go. I was overwhelmed with emotion. When I talked with him on the way to the hospital, he said he had already made his peace that he was going to die. When he grabbed my hand, it changed that course for him mentally. Suddenly he had a sense of hope. He had such a strong grip on my hand I was almost falling in on top of him. Having that bond with him, just through his hand, that was powerful to me. I was able to give him hope." The boys were treated for serious hypothermia, but ultimately recovered completely.

"We do that with a dementia patient who is afraid, afraid of everything, and we hold their hand and we tell them they're safe. Those sorts of things are so important. It seems like between the hours of three and four in the morning is when people are the loneliest. A lot of times when I see people in the early morning, they mostly just need someone to talk to. They're dealing with their pain and they just can't deal with it anymore or they just need emotional healing. Holding onto someone's hand, whether it be in a snowbank or on a stretcher is really important, reassuring them and giving them a sense of hope that everything is going to be okay."

"Firefighting is still very much a man's job at least culturally. There's a feeling that if you're a woman you have to emulate that, you have to be this brute, physical force person. And I just challenge that. It takes a lot of different people to perform the job. We all have strengths and weaknesses and we all bring those things to the table. If we can work with that, we make a great team."

Shelia Vitalis

Shelia Vitalis at live burn training

# The Murder of a Child

In the spring of 2011, Shelia Vitalis was preparing to deploy for the second time to Iraq as an Army reservist. She will be stationed there for a year as a military police officer. Here in the United States, Shelia is a career fire captain with the Durham County, North Carolina Fire Department, where she has served since 2001.

Prior to joining this department, Shelia was a firefighter with the City of Durham Fire Department for three years. She served in the Army full time from 1986 to 1991 and then did "odd jobs. I didn't have a career. There wasn't anything I wanted to do for the rest of my life. I never imagined being a firefighter. Growing up, I always thought firefighters were kind of silly. Why would you go into a burning building? Now here I am."

Shelia remembered a particularly harrowing medical call she responded to. "We went to a call that came in as a cardiac arrest of a seven year old boy. A seven year old boy in cardiac arrest? I thought maybe the dispatcher made a mistake, and maybe it was someone who was seventy. But when we got there, we found out it was indeed a seven year old, and that his father had killed him."

"His mom and two other kids were still in the house. The father had tried to kill them also, but they were bigger and older and they were able to fight him off. The mom was crying and looking at me with these eyes that said, help me. But there was nothing we could do."

"They sent all of us to counseling afterward. It affected all of us because most of us have kids. I have a kid, and a grandbaby. Just to see that kid there and be so helpless; it affected us for weeks, for months. Still to this day, to think about it, I tear up a little bit. Even on the scene I had to go around to the back of the house and let my emotions go. It was awful."

"The dad was upstairs and we had to go up and help him. He had tried to kill himself too and had stabbed himself three or four times, in the neck and the stomach. So in addition to having to move the child, we had to go up and put the dad on a stretcher and bring him down. Blood was everywhere. And I know it's wrong to think this way but we all thought, why are we helping him? He did this to that little boy. He survived. It was hard to treat him knowing what he had done. But they tell you in all the EMT and fire classes, you have to do your job. We helped him to survive, but we could not help the little boy."

"I had never been to a scene where a child was murdered. He just looked like he was sleeping. He had been strangled with bare hands. The mom wanted to come to the station and tell everyone thank you a few weeks later, but the crew couldn't face her. So I said, okay, I'll do it, I'm not going to let the lady down because right now she's reaching out. She wanted some closure. So I talked to her, and then the whole neighborhood had a gathering for the little boy with food, drinks, and a 5K run. I went and I did the 5K run for him. The mom came over and gave me a hug and she was crying, and that made me get emotional too."

"As hard as it was, it helped me a lot to see her. She was trying to move on with her life; she had to, because she has two other kids to take care of. She was probably putting on an act for the kids, but I could feel her emotion when she gave me that hug. She almost broke down crying. I wanted to tell her it would be okay, but I don't know that it will be okay for her. I hope so. But I don't know."

"The thing I am most proud of is that we get so much respect—from little kids, from women that see me on the truck. It's a male dominated field. But I think any woman can do this job if she chooses to. Serving my community gives me a lot of self worth. Everybody thinks I'm a hero, especially my family."

"I want my son and my grandchildren to know that they can be anything they want to be. I want to make a path for kids growing up today, male or female, to make it easier for them. People come up to me, strangers, little kids. I get a lot of questions. They ask me, how hard is it, and are you afraid? And I tell them, I am afraid sometimes, but I have a job to do, and you can do the same thing if you set your mind to it."

Chassity Pollard

Chassity Pollard at Get Out Alive training

# Small Sadness

Chassity Pollard has been a firefighter with the Karns Volunteer Fire Department outside of Knoxville, Tennessee since 2008. Prior to joining this fire department, Chassity also served with the Creston Fire Department in Ohio. A former Army reservist, Chassity works as a lab technician, as well as being the mother of a four year old daughter. Chassity's father, also a volunteer, inspired her to become a firefighter.

Firefighters experience many types of incidents in their work—the big fire, the dramatic multi-car accident. But sometimes it is the smaller, quieter calls that really stick with them. Chassity remembered one such incident.

"We went on a call to a lady who was having trouble breathing. When we got there, we found out that her family knew that she was dying of lung cancer. But they hadn't told her yet, so she didn't know that she was dying. The woman was in her sixties, and she knew she was sick, but she didn't know that the doctors had given her just a few weeks to live. She had no idea that her time left was so short. Being there and knowing that about her just made me realize that we sometimes take life for granted when we really shouldn't. We don't know how long we really have."

"Being there with her that day made me appreciate my own life more, and reminded me to live life to its fullest. Life is short and being on the fire department makes me realize that everything can change in the blink of an eye. You just don't know. Now, every time we go out on a call, it crosses my mind—the uncertainty of it—that the people we will see don't know what's going to happen and we don't know what we're going to come up on. We could be on a routine fire, but stuff happens to firefighters all the time. They think they're going back to the station, and sometimes they don't."

"For me being a firefighter is a huge accomplishment because obviously it's a male dominated sort of job, at least the way most people see it. I feel like I keep up with the guys. It's hard sometimes, because they sometimes do think you're the weaker person, kind of like the last person picked for the team. But as long as I keep up and do what I need to do, I'm just like the guys."

Maria Figueroa

Maria Figueroa as a young recruit

## Mother Mary

When Maria Figueroa was a little girl growing up in Cuba, one of her uncles was a volunteer firefighter. She remembers that "watching my uncle run to the firehouse and drive away in the fire truck was quite thrilling." Still, Maria never imagined herself doing the job. Years later, as an adult in Miami, Maria was struggling as the single mother of a two year old. "I am a domestic violence survivor. I left my abusive husband and was struggling to make ends meet. I had only a high school education, was working two jobs, and collecting food stamps."

Maria started thinking she should look for a "man's job" because she knew those kinds of jobs paid more. She decided to join the police department and began serving as a reserve officer. But then she met the man who would become her second husband, who was a firefighter with the Miami-Dade Fire Department. "He and his friends recruited me to become a firefighter instead. Never in a million years had I considered it before, but I applied, took the test, did great on my interview, and was hired." That was in 1983, and as Maria says, "the rest is history."

Maria served on the Miami-Dade Fire Department until her retirement as a captain in 2008. Along the way, she completed a four year college degree and many certifications. Currently she is the Regional Director of the Fire Prevention Field Office of the National Fire Protection Association (NFPA). In this position, Maria advocates for fire prevention and life safety systems and education, and especially for fire sprinklers in all new construction. "I thrived in my fire department career, and now have a successful career with NFPA after retirement. It is true what they say: Success is the best revenge."

Firefighters always have to be resourceful and Maria remembered a medical call that required quick and creative thinking on her part. "It was a call for a person with a mental health history who was drowning. We arrived to find a man in the middle of his pool, obviously psychotic and mumbling nonsensically. He would go under the water for awhile and then come back up. The police were there also but we all felt that it was dangerous to go in to get him and instead tried to talk him out of the pool. This went on for about ten minutes while we all devised a plan of attack."

"Then suddenly the man said, 'I am Jesus and I am going to pour my blood for you.' He was just talking to everyone in general. Just as suddenly it occurred to me to say, 'I am your mother Mary and I command you to get out of the pool, my son.' We all looked at each other but sure enough, he got out of the pool and followed my commands to get on the stretcher while others secured him."

"Of course we didn't want to laugh in front of his relatives, but afterward we gathered outside with the cops and we laughed so hard. I was known after that as Mother Mary and every time the cops would see me coming, they would say, Hey, here comes Mother Mary! But it worked!"

Maria believes that her fire service career made her a better person, stronger and more mature. However, she also notes that, "I paid a very high physical and emotional price for being on the job those 25 years. But I am proud that I served the community that became my hometown after leaving my home country of Cuba, and I am proud that I fought many visible and important battles early in my career to defend gender equality in the fire service. I had to work extra hard to earn respect and live down the troublemaker label."

"When I was fighting those battles in the 1980s and 1990s for equal treatment, for better fitting equipment, for maternity and sexual harassment policies, I wanted my legacy to be that if my daughter wanted to join the fire service, she would find a place much different from the one I found when I joined in 1983." In this regard, Maria's dream may have come true. "My daughter did not choose to become a firefighter, but a friend's daughter did, and recently told her mother that she knows that all the benefits she enjoys today she owes in part to me, because she knows how hard I fought for them."

Annie Webb

## Parking Lot Delivery

Annie Webb was a professional opera singer when she became a firefighter with Cobb County, Georgia in 2009. She started voice lessons at age thirteen and eventually obtained a master's degree in opera performance. While singing professionally, Annie also worked as a personal trainer, and met firefighters at a gym where she worked part time. For her, opera and firefighting are not completely dissimilar, especially regarding the lack of a 9-5 schedule. "There are very few jobs out there that allow you that freedom, and also serve a real purpose."

One thing Annie likes about being a firefighter is that she learns something new every shift. "There is so much truth to the fact that we're a jack of all trades and master of none in this field. We're the catch-all. We do it all. If the police can't do it and the EMS service can't do it, and utility can't do it, then call the fire department, because they'll do it. That means we're up on all the new technology with hybrid vehicles, and the physics of fire behavior, and medical terminology and technology. It's a constant challenge."

Annie's most memorable medical call occurred not long after she graduated from recruit school. "I was stationed at a location in the county not known for its call volume. I was on the engine, and we were mobile, on our way back to the station. We heard a call on the radio for another truck to respond to an obstetrics (OB) call for a 29 year old woman with a cardiac history, contractions one minute apart, in the parking lot of a Publix grocery store."

Because her engine was closer, they responded to the call along with the truck that had been dispatched. "I had passed the EMT registry just a month and half earlier. The last thing we covered in school was childbirth and delivery. I'd never even seen childbirth and didn't have kids of my own to relate the experience to. In my brain, I was frantically trying to remember what comes first, but the guy next to me said, remember, women have been doing this for thousands of years. We're going to catch and that's about it."

"We pulled into the parking lot about the same time as the rescue unit arrived. The medic and I ran to the pregnant woman. The first thing we noticed was that she had a big scar on her chest from previous heart surgery. The medic asked her, how far along are you and do you feel the need to push? And she screamed, thirty-seven weeks, and YES!"

Annie's crew looked around the parking lot but the only place to deliver the baby was on the bed of the pregnant woman's pickup truck. "A couple of the older guys were not keen to be up close on this call, so they took the twenty foot pike poles and made a screen from tarps to provide a wall for privacy. It was eight in the morning and the parking lot was busy. The woman and her mother had been stuck in Atlanta morning traffic, and the young woman suddenly told her mother, you need to pull over, I'm delivering this baby now."

"We laid out the OB kit and got the woman onto the truck bed. She was wearing a tank top, plaid maternity shorts, and flip flops. The paramedic grabbed the shorts and I just have this memory of those plaid shorts and a black thong flying across the parking lot. The medic took a look and confirmed the baby was crowning. We stood in position and she pushed—once, twice—shoulder out! Three times—head was out and we suctioned. Then once more, and that baby was born."

"I've never seen anything so amazing. Childbirth is dirty, messy, gross, and wonderful. It wasn't until that moment that I knew for sure I'd be able to handle myself with all the EMS calls that come along. I kept my head. Helping deliver that baby gave me amazing confidence." Two weeks later, the mother brought the baby, a healthy little girl, to meet the firefighters who had helped her enter the world.

"I've always wanted to help people change their lives. Now that I see what goes on out in the world, I am far more concerned about my friends and family and their safety. I've always been an athlete, but this job gives purpose to my gym time. It drives my workouts, and helps me be a more effective personal trainer in my part time job, because I know first hand the importance of strength for women. I am most proud that I have proved that women can do this job."

"I hope my legacy will be helping my county and showing little girls that there's nothing they can't do. Most important to me is teaching my colleagues the importance of taking care of themselves both inside and outside the fire station through exercise and proper nutrition." And even though Annie's life is now about being a firefighter, she had not completely left her old life behind. "Once they found out that I can sing, I end up singing at all the recruit class graduations."

# Chapter 6

## Station Life

It is hard to describe how wonderful it is to be a firefighter on a crew that really meshes together as a team. On the emergency scene, such good chemistry makes for smooth operations, the so-called "good fire," when everything clicks and crew members don't even need to speak to communicate effectively.

But being a firefighter is much more than fighting fires, and most of the time is spent in the company of coworkers in the station or performing routine duties. It is under these circumstances that crew cohesion is really tested. Whereas a large fire tends to bring out the best in everyone and allows petty differences to fall away, routine station life can either be a great joy or a real drag, depending on the crew.

Firefighters live together in close quarters, so there are plenty of opportunities to get on each others' nerves. There will always be the snorer in the dorm, or the guy who leaves toenail clippings on the carpet, or the firefighter who monopolizes the bathroom first thing in the morning, or the person who eats the other shift's food. As in a family, the keys to overcoming such small problems are humor, patience, the ability to confront without anger, and most of all, a recognition of the greater underlying common mission that joins people together.

Getting along is part of the job, and firefighters who make the effort to get along and bring out the best in their coworkers reap many rewards. Station life among a good crew is some of the best fun you'll ever have, and on some shifts it seems like you never stop laughing.

One of the great things about firefighters is that they are responsible adults who have not forgotten how to play. The nature of the job demands humor as therapy at times, and some of the darker humor that serves that purpose probably would not be understood by the general public. But if you've just returned to quarters after responding to the third suicide that week, a little rude humor is sometimes just the thing.

Firefighters have many traditions that serve to bond a crew together. Most fire crews still eat meals together, and for many, sharing food is a highlight of the day. As Diana Herndon of the Iona-McGregor, Florida Fire Department observed, "We always eat together. There are crews on my department that don't eat together but for me it is such an important part of what we do. We're living with these people for a third of our lives. It's like sitting down with your family at home. It definitely makes me feel like I'm appreciated and wanted around the station." Firefighters are on duty 24 hours a day, 365 days a year, so on holidays when others are with families and friends, fire stations often pull out all the stops with shared feasts.

Nicknames are another fire service tradition. When I first came on the job, I remember being sent to cover an outlying station, and my captain and engineer spent the two hours we were there going over the department roster and telling me everyone's nicknames. It was enormously beneficial information to have, as I had been hearing for weeks about people without knowing who they actually were. I still have that paper somewhere with "Stretch" and "Hap" and "Grapey" and "Smiley" scrawled on it.

A well-crafted practical joke can be legendary within a fire department. There was the rubber cake delivered as a supposed gift from a citizen at Christmastime, the prank calls by one firefighter to others in the same station, the plastic snake. One guy bought a scary rubber mask and went to great lengths (including hiding in a locker for half an hour) to scare others on his shift with it. Practical jokes that were inclusive in spirit were always appreciated, even if you happened to be the brunt of one that day.

Individual crews develop their own traditions. At one station, we played along with Jeopardy every night, and tried to guess the Final Jeopardy answer just from the category (if you got it, you won.) We played (and cheated at) Trivial Pursuit and did crosswords as a team; we worked out as a group to Jane Fonda aerobics videos (even though half the guys never forgave her for the 1970s). A couple guys took up oil painting with the TV painter Bob Ross, while another built birdhouses after hours in the station.

If you worked an overtime shift, you were expected to buy a food treat for the shift—traditionally doughnuts, but sometimes ice cream, pie, cake, or gourmet muffins. Rites of passage (promotions, the end of probation) might be celebrated with a trip to Dairy Queen for Blizzards. Popcorn, often with special seasoned salt, was the evening snack of choice at many fire stations.

Hot days often meant water fights while washing the rig. Some departments still have a tradition of "bucketing" new recruits— dousing them with a bucket of water from a hidden high location when they least expect it.

Shifts working at the same station often have rivalries, either real or just for fun. The task of painting the station might lead to shift-war graffiti while the job was in process ("C Shift Rules!" becoming "C Shift DRooles!") Sometimes a crew from one station would sneak into another station when they knew that crew was out and play some joke, then deny knowledge of it. Such covert operations could lead to months of paybacks and increasingly creative ways of messing with the other crew.

For the most part, the joking around was all in fun, and served a real purpose—to solidify the team, to provide a relief valve for otherwise stressful days, and just to have fun. The fire station can be a lonely or miserable place to be with a group of people who don't get along, but when it works, days at the firehouse are some of the best times you'll ever have.

Meg Richardson

Meg Richardson instructing a live fire exercise

# Practical Jokes

Meg Richardson joined the Marietta, Georgia Fire Department in 1997 after a first career as a human resources and training director. Currently a company officer, Meg is married to a captain with the Atlanta Fire Department. It was her husband who suggested she make the career move to the fire department. "I laughed. I told him I'm the executive type, not a firefighter. But he was coming home smelling of smoke and he was happy, and I was coming home stressed out after working sixty hours a week. So I started thinking about it." And now? "I would prefer to go into a burning building any day versus working in the corporate world."

One of the things that Meg most values about her life in the fire service is the strong sense of camaraderie she feels with her fellow firefighters. "Firefighting is the ultimate team sport. When that team is working, and we're fighting a fire, we don't even really have to speak." Meg talked about the role of humor as a way of building strong teams. "A lighter arena is just much more comfortable to work in. We're not allowed to horseplay—there's been a rule about that since the early 1990s. But there are still a lot of practical jokes. You need to be the first to laugh at yourself."

One of the funniest jokes that Meg recalled was very simple. "After an arduous training event that spanned the course of several shifts, we found a large white cooler sitting in the engine bay at our main fire station. That station houses an engine, a ladder truck, a heavy rescue and the shift chief, so on any given day there are about ten folks on duty. During the shift change, every time a new person reported in, he would pass by this cooler that had a sign on it reading: Free sodas. Help yourself."

"Firefighters can't refuse free food, so nearly everyone opened the cooler to help himself to a cool refreshing beverage. Unfortunately, what he found instead was a large rubber snake attached by a piece of fishing line to the inside of the lid. When a person opened the lid, the snake would spring out, inevitably extracting a high pitched yelp from the terrified person. This of course was to the delight of the growing crowd of firefighters, most who had just fallen for the prank!"

Meg admits that she has often been the one to instigate such pranks. "There was a guy who was terrified of spiders. Think of all the crawl spaces we have to go into, filled with snakes and spiders and rats. So one shift when we were working together, I took a piece of dental floss and one of those big plastic spiders, so when he pulled down his sleeping bag in his bed, the spider would pull out from under his pillow. He screamed like a little kid, but thought it was hilarious."

"Everyone here knows my professional background, and in some ways I tend to keep a distance when at work. So they never suspect it's me playing these jokes. One time we had a guy that was super lazy and never paid his house dues on time. So we took his TV remote hostage and hid it and sent him on a scavenger hunt to find it. At the end there was a kidnapping letter that said, you won't get your remote back until you pay your house dues. But nobody knew who did it, and that was half the fun."

A self-described "fitness and nutrition fanatic," Meg is committed to making the fire service healthier and safer in the long run. "I teach regularly on these topics, both in the formal classroom setting and in the firehouse. Personally I want to stay strong for as long as I can. I will strive in the remainder of my career to maintain and set the example for fitness for duty. I want to be instrumental in introducing our fire staff to nutrition and fitness practices that will enhance their quality of life now and after retirement. That, I hope, will be my legacy."

Carol Murphy

Carol Murphy on her last day at work

# Giving as Good as You Get

Carol Murphy was a dispatcher when she was hired as a firefighter with the Lexington, Massachusetts Fire Department in 1989. For most of her career, Carol was the only woman on her department. She was thrown into the job from Day One. "After I graduated from the fire academy, I came back to the station and I started driver's training right away. They usually don't do that, but they needed drivers." Carol fit in easily with station life, and understood the offerings of acceptance given to her. "Everyone gets a nickname, so everyone started calling me Murph. Nicknames are good. Some of them maybe can't be said in polite company, but for the most part, they are a sign of affection and acceptance."

Part of Carol's success on the job was her ability to give as good as she got. She remembered one incident linked to her crew's early realization that she was not going to meet their stereotypes of what women could do. "Being the only woman on the job, they figured I could cook. So they showed me the kitchen and shut the doors on me. I don't know how to cook but they didn't know that. So I said, I can't cook. What am I doing in here? I can't even boil water!"

"I started banging pans around and screaming and making howling noises like a devil and I tried to get out. And they said, Don't let her out of the kitchen! She's going nuts! I was sweating and my hair was a mess, and I had pans all over the floor. They came in and said, We told you to cook! And I said, I don't know how to cook. You don't want me in the kitchen. It's true—I make crispy rice and I burn the English muffins, and when the guys finally realized what I was saying was true, they said, You really suck at this! Get the hell out of the kitchen! But I do great clean up."

Sometime later, a man from another shift was transferred into Carol's station to work with her and her officer, a good friend who had just been promoted to lieutenant. This new guy "thought he was a big funny guy, a wise guy, so he said, to me, You're going in the kitchen and we're going to make you cook. And I said to him, Oh! You used the 'C' word in front of me! Then I thought—this is good, I have a new lieutenant, I can get back at him. He had done something to me a long time before, and I never got back at him for it. So I wrote the word 'cook' on a piece of paper and folded it in half. Then I went to my officer and said very seriously, Lieutenant, I need to talk to you. I have a problem. It's the new kid, Derek. My lieutenant said, Let's go in the kitchen to talk."

"So we went in the kitchen and shut all the doors and he asked me what happened. I said, He said a bad word in front of me, and I slid the piece of paper with the word 'cook' on it across the table, but my officer couldn't see what was written on it. I told him, He said that to me. And my lieutenant was turning white and starting to sweat bullets.

"He told me later, Oh my God, here I was, a brand new lieutenant and you're going to file a sexual harassment complaint with me. What am I going to do? So he opened up the piece of paper and he looked at the word and I could see smoke coming out of his ears. He said, I thought you said he said the bad word! And I said, Well, that's the other bad word. This is THE bad word. So he started laughing and said, You almost gave me heart failure! I'm a brand new lieutenant and I don't know what I'm doing and I think you're going to file a sexual harassment suit!"

"Then he told me to leave the room and to go tell Derek he wanted to see him. So Derek went to his office and the others outside all wanted to know what was going on, because they had heard us laughing. So I told them and we all had our ears to the door. The officer told Derek, Carol has filed a sexual harassment complaint. And Derek was backpedaling—But I didn't say anything! The officer said, Did you say this word to her? And he slid the paper across to him. And then I heard: Murphy, you're dead! And we were all out there laughing our asses off. It was the funniest thing, because I got the both of them the same day. And no one ever asked me to cook again!"

"Being a firefighter has made me stronger. I'm not the shy, quiet person I once was. I'm not afraid to go eyeball to eyeball with someone. I'm not afraid to speak my mind. I have a lot more self-confidence that I never had before. I'm very proud to say I'm a firefighter, because I worked hard for it. Nobody gave me the job. I earned it."

"I hope the guys will remember me as someone who was funny and easy to get along with. I look at things differently now than a civilian does. When I'm driving, I'm constantly aware and listening for sirens, noticing the little strobe light over the intersection that's flashing, meaning an emergency vehicle is about to come through. I drive more defensively. It's made me a better person overall. But I never did learn how to cook!"

Susan Salinger

Susan Salinger and her crew

# Caking

Susan Salinger was 35 when she was hired with the San Jose,
California Fire Department in 1988. Prior to joining the fire service,
Susan worked in a number of fields: "If you name a job, I probably
did it—landscaping, construction, waitressing, teaching swimming
and aerobics, among others." Susan had a degree in art and was
working as a paramedic for an ambulance company when she made
the move to the fire department. Susan retired in 2011 as a battalion
chief. She is looking forward to community volunteer work and
starting an art studio now that her fire department career is behind
her.

Susan felt that being a battalion chief was the position that suited her the best on the fire department. "I was older when I started the job, with two kids, and it just kind of irked me to have these younger guys ordering me around. I worked really hard to promote. I took the battalion chief's test twice and the second time I took it, I came in first on the list. So nobody could say that I got promoted because I was a woman, or anything like that. Being a battalion chief is a job with considerable autonomy, so I got to do it my way." Among the changes Susan initiated were goal setting and mentoring for company officers, and group hikes and bikes rides on off days to gain area familiarization in the wildland urban interface.

Susan has fond memories of station life on the San Jose Fire Department. "I was an engineer, and had maybe been on the job six years at that point. I was at a station that was known for being a tough guy station. It was my birthday, and they caked me. That's when they give you a birthday cake and smash it in your face, which is what they would do for people they liked."

"First they run around the station trying to get you with it, and then they smear it all over you. It was chocolate ganache and it went up my nose and was all in my hair. Then we immediately had a fire call, so we had to go and had no time to clean up. You just shove your helmet on your head and hope nobody notices. I was always kind of a prankster myself, but as you go up in rank, you can't participate in that so much. But it was so much fun."

"Being a firefighter taught me how to be in the moment. We went to so many things where everybody was just going along in their daily life and then suddenly someone dies, or their house burns down, or they get hit by a tree limb, or their car goes off into the canal. You never think things like that are going to happen."

"So many people spend most of their lives worrying about what happened in the past, or what will happen in the future, that they never get to enjoy the moment. And it's really all that we have. That's what we would always say to each other after we would go to one of those tragic calls: Enjoy life. Enjoy every moment."

"Everyone has to prove themselves when they get to the next rank, and I think this is more true for women than men. I think I did this, and not just to them, but to myself as well, while always being true to myself. I was able to mentor a couple other women who later promoted, and I really like that I was able to help them."

"You have to be able to say you don't know the answer. I've seen so many times when people were bluffing and it never works out. In my battalion, I was able to make asking for help an accepted part of working together. I showed them it was okay to do things differently, to be more creative. I want people to say that I got the job done, and we had fun doing it."

Sarah Twomey

Sarah Twomey after a three alarm fire

# Nicknames

Sarah Twomey has been a volunteer with the Leadington Fire
Department since 2010. Her department serves the small town of
Leadington and mutual aid areas around an hour south of St. Louis,
Missouri. Sarah works full time as an EMT for Iron County
Ambulance, based in a small community an hour south of her home.
She is married and is the mother of a young son.

After Sarah obtained her EMT license she decided she also wanted to
be a firefighter. "I put my application in at two different departments
and the one that called me first is the one that interviewed me, and
they asked me to join right on the spot."

Sarah remembers the first months on the job. "When we have new firefighters join, they're put on a ninety day probation period. If you do well, you're allowed to turn in your pager for a radio. It's one of the main things that changes when you go from being a probie to being an actual firefighter."

Before that critical ninety day period was up for Sarah, she experienced an aspect of station life that made her feel like a full member of the crew. "I remember going to the firehouse one day and the chief had me go into his office. I thought, okay, I must be in trouble. I went in there, and he said, Give me your pager. So I gave it to him, and in turn, he gave me a radio. I guess I was excited and relieved so when I walked out of his office with my new radio in my hand, I yelled, Woot, woot! It's just something I say when I get excited but everyone got a kick out of it."

"A day or so later, we got a call. We were all gearing up as fast as we could and as I put on my bunkers, I turned my helmet around to put it on, and on the back of my helmet in stick-on letters was 'Woot Woot.' Everyone else started cracking up, because they'd all had a part in it. It really made me feel needed and a part of the crew. From that day forward, my name isn't Sarah or 3924 in the firehouse, it's Woot Woot, or Woot for short. When I go on mutual aid calls, they call me Woot. I'm not even sure that they know my real first name."

"I am proud to be a woman doing this job. There are a lot of girls, they'd rather wear their stilettos, but I'd rather be in bunker boots and in the firehouse. It's important that we have women doing it to say, we're not just a housewife or a mom. We can serve the community just as well as any man."

"I hope people that I work with or people in my family see that this work is my passion. I think it always will be. I hope they see that every day we put our lives on the line to help other people."

"I got married very young, right out of high school. Then after we had our son, I was a stay-at-home mom, and I worked at a gas station. I was really kind of a nobody. But then I got into EMS and I felt needed. I feel proud. It's a good feeling to know you were there to help somebody."

Karrie Leigh Boswell

Karrie Leigh Boswell speaking at an International Association of Fire Fighters Conference

# Good Leadership

Karrie Leigh Boswell has been a firefighter since she was a child, literally. Leigh (as she is known) participated in her high school's cadet program and knew at the age of sixteen that she wanted to be a firefighter/paramedic. She graduated from high school in June 1987, and in February 1988, she was in recruit school with the Fairfax County, Virginia Fire Department. Being a firefighter was part of growing up for Leigh. At the beginning, "I thought I knew it all. I was just a girl with braces when I started recruit school and I thought I was **it**."

"In recruit school you had to keep your shoes shined and your uniforms pressed and if you didn't, you had to do pushups or whatever. Two weeks before the end of recruit school I came into work and my shoes weren't shined properly. The instructors were giving me grief during line up that my shoes looked bad. And I was so naïve and stupid that I made the mistake of saying that my dad was out of town, and so he didn't get a chance to shine them."

"I didn't think anything of it. Every night my mother would iron my shirt and pants, and have them hanging up for me in the laundry room. I had two pairs of shoes and my dad would shine them. So there were the other recruits, they go home at night and have sick kids. They had a life. I was a child. I'm lucky I didn't get killed!"

"I don't believe that without the structure and discipline of the fire service I would have ever remained so focused in my adult life. I know that I would never have had such financial security. A woman in today's workforce without a college education simply cannot earn the kind of money that we do in the fire department." Leigh is currently a lieutenant with the Fairfax County Fire Department and president of the department's women's association. She is also active with her local union and the International Association of Fire Fighters at the national level.

Leigh talked about the importance of leadership in developing crew unity and high morale and performance. "My current station is the most awesome team of firefighters that I have ever worked with. The foundation for this is our leader, our captain. In the fire service, crew unity and situational awareness save lives. This starts at the station level and begins with leaders who promote a feeling that every shift member is unique, adds value, and has an equal voice. This environment is what gives us all the confidence on the scene of an emergency incident to say things like, Captain, I think you should look at the roof before we go in."

"In a paramilitary organization like the fire service, chain of command can be tricky in the sense that to question orders must be done in such a manner that you do not appear insubordinate. On a daily basis a leader who works to build team unity, comfortable interaction among members, and the confidence for each member to ask questions is a leader whose worth is not easily measured."

Leigh described several ways that her captain builds a sense of team among the crew: "Physical training is done as a group, we have dish games every night, movies are watched together, shift parties, and so on." Each shift begins with a coin spin game, a tradition that some fire departments have adopted from the military as a way of building team identity. "In the military, a general or a specific group would have their own coin. At our station, we have a station coin. When we end our morning line up each shift, we get in a circle around a table. You put your coin on its edge and spin it. And if yours falls off the table, you have to do fourteen pushups, because our station number is fourteen. Then you can make rules for the game, like no pointing, no talking, no laughing. It's fun, and builds camaraderie."

"I have worked in many stations and this is not always the environment that exists. The value of this kind of leadership is more specific to me as a woman. We have to feel safe. Every time we go to a new station, we have to prove our worth again. We have to feel that if we say something or do something, we're not going to be ridiculed and harassed, beyond what is just normal in the fire service. You have to have a comfort level."

"I think that's one of the major barriers in breaking down the glass ceilings in some of the upper ranks in the fire service. Women just don't have the confidence. They don't have officers that are encouraging them and telling them: You can do this, you can break through. Women get to a certain position, whether it's driver or company officer, and they feel safe, because they've mastered that. When you work in a station where your worth is measured not by the fact that you look like everyone else, talk like everyone else or even think like everyone else but instead for the way you actually look, talk and think, then you are really part of a crew that is destined to do some amazing things."

"My legacy is pretty simple. I am most proud of the service that I provide to people who call 911. Everyone in the fire service must remember that our image in the public eye can be won or lost in one instant. We have a dark humor about us as it relates to our profession. We laugh at things that others find horrific. But we must always remember who the customer is and that they deserve to be treated with the utmost dignity and respect even when they have done something silly to get themselves in the position they are currently in. The eighteen year old college student who has gotten so drunk that he can't hold his head up is no different from the sixty year old grandmother who can't breathe."

"I never, ever take for granted how much impact I can have in one person's life in one moment. I would like my legacy to be that I was funny, took great care of patients, and fought hard every day to better the working conditions of firefighters."

# Chapter 7

## Overcoming Obstacles

All women firefighters have faced obstacles in the job. For some, these challenges are merely inconvenient or annoying, such as always having to tailor pants to get them to fit, or putting up with occasional incredulous stares or odd comments from members of the public. Women as firefighters are still unusual, making up less than 5% of the total number of firefighters. Some women serve as the only woman on their department for their entire careers. There are still some fire departments that have yet to hire their first woman.

On the lowest level, obstacles facing women might even seem funny at times. One woman told the story of an experience at a fire scene: "Once I was operating a pump on a working fire when a woman walked past. Seeing me standing next to my pump, she asked, Do you drive that truck? I was feeling proud when I answered her question yes, until she followed immediately with, Don't they let girls go inside?"

Another woman commented, "It is maddening when someone says to me that females cannot be firefighters, and they doubt that I would be able to rescue them in an emergency. I proceed to tell them that I would be able to and that it doesn't matter if I am female or male. In almost all of my training where it has come to rescuing someone I have been paired up with someone twice my size, if not more. So I know I can do it."

More serious obstacles await many women who pursue firefighting either as a career or a volunteer vocation. Poorly fitting safety gear, facilities designed for only one gender, lack of consideration for pregnancy—these things all impact women directly. "At first my boots were a problem," said one woman. "I wear a size six men's boot and they didn't make fire boots that small. I had to stuff socks in the ends of the toes to keep them on." Another woman commented that she'd had few problems on her department, but "there is no maternity policy in place. I'm getting married soon and want to have children. It worries me not knowing what will happen."

By far the toughest obstacle that women face as firefighters is negativity from their coworkers that may range from doubt to outright hostility. "I haven't had a lot of obstacles in my career compared to a lot of women I know," said one woman. "If I had to pick one that irritated me it would be having my opinion devalued because a woman 'wouldn't know about that.' If I could prove them wrong on the spot, I'd push them aside and prove it. One time it was as simple as taking over the driver's seat of an old stick shift pumper. A guy couldn't get it into gear because he didn't realize you had to double clutch it. I hopped in and happily drove it back to the station."

Some problems are not so easily resolved. Women firefighters have been shunned by coworkers, set up to fail, directly harassed, and even threatened. Such treatment is the exception, but common enough that many women have had to develop strategies for dealing with it. "When I first came on the job, every time I worked with a different crew, I felt like I had to prove myself all over again. I think for most guys once you get out of the fire academy the assumption is that you can do the job until you manage to prove that you can't. I believe the reverse is true for women: you can't do the job until you prove that you can. I dealt with this by always being the first person to step up when a task such as lifting a cot, stretching hose, or forcing entry needed to be done."

Another woman commented, "I had to work harder than the men, to prove myself over and over again. Some of my male co-workers, though not all, played games on the fire ground and in the firehouse to purposely get the women to quit, and some did just that. Early in my career I realized that if I am going to fight this battle, there would be some basic steps that I would need to put in place. First and foremost, I learned how to be safe while I was there. Then I learned the department's rules and regulations like the back of my hand, so I would know what they could or couldn't do to me. Last but not least, it is very important that you stand up for yourself, stand your ground."

In addition to developing an action plan to deal with adversity, women also had to learn to be patient and persistent. "When I first started with a particular group, they ignored me and did not include me in certain things. They had to include me in training, but they ignored me around the station—did not ask what I wanted for lunch or supper after they had all ordered food, or did not include me in some off-duty things. I put up with it for the few months I was with that group, and then I was transferred and everything was fine. I have gained a huge amount of patience working on this job."

It may take years for some women to break down the barriers placed before them by others. "The first ten years I was on the job, I had a lot of obstacles and there was a lot of hatred and nasty acts directed at me personally. I had done nothing to these people to cause them to hate me. They just had an idea in their heads about what I was like even though they did not know me and had never had a conversation with me. I always felt that what I was doing was for the betterment of the entire fire service, not just to allow women to become firefighters. When people are allowed to bring their genuine selves to the job, the organization benefits from that. But even at the worst times, I loved the job so much that I was not going to quit just because some people decided I should not be in the job. I was a good firefighter. Why should people who did not even know me get the final say on whether I should be a firefighter or not?"

Finally, overcoming obstacles and developing real relationships on the job often involves forgiveness. It is not enough to just constantly prove your worth to others, which is an exhausting task that eventually leads to cynicism, burnout, and attrition. Some women have been truly wronged by others on the job, but they also realize that individuals make mistakes, redemption is possible, and being true to themselves is more important than proving themselves to others.

One woman said, "The most significant obstacle I faced was being generally ostracized just because I was a woman. At first I became angry and walked around with a chip on my shoulder. Then I grew wiser and threw away the chip, but continued to fight the good fight professionally. As a result, I thrived in my career, gaining recognition from inside and outside the organization." Another woman observed, "I realized the loudest negative voice I needed to quiet was the one in my head. Making it over that hurdle allowed me to be a part of the crew and just do my job."

In the end, self-acceptance may be the hardest goal to achieve. One woman said, "I felt that I had to be as close to perfect as possible. I was afraid that any mistake that I made would be attributed to the fact that I was a woman and that other women firefighters would somehow pay the price along with me. It took many years before I accepted the fact that none of us, male or female, are infallible and that it wasn't fair to hold myself or other women firefighters to greater scrutiny, whether or not others may do so. I needed to learn how to forgive myself of my mistakes, to learn from them, and to continue to move forward. I think that it was when I became an officer and I saw young firefighters struggle with their mistakes and the criticisms of others that I learned we truly were all in this boat together and that my position as a woman firefighter was not so unique in that regard."

Positive action, courageous tenacity, and forgiveness of oneself and others—these are key components of success for women as firefighters. In this section, three women tell stories about how these characteristics and values allowed them not only to endure, but to attain great success, and the position of chief.

Katherine Ridenhour and her crew

Katherine Ridenhour

# Action

In 1986, Katherine Ridenhour was training to become a professional bodyguard when she became a cadet with the Greeley, Colorado Fire Department. "That training was invaluable for me in the fire service from the standpoint of the mental aspects of the job. It helped me not only prepare for my own promotional processes, but also how to teach people to prepare for promotion." Katherine moved to the Aurora, Colorado Fire Department in 1989, where she retired as a battalion chief in 2010. When asked about her post-retirement plans, Katherine says, "I still feel like I have a lot to give back, more than I can ever repay. I hope to give back through teaching, especially in the area of strategy and tactics. The fire service needs good, sound, common sense tactics that will keep us safe."

Katherine loved every aspect of her fire service career, but said, "The best part of my career was being a chief. I had such great officers and firefighters. Even some of the greatest challenges I had as a chief which involved giving out discipline—every one of those people became some of the dearest people I had. Every time I had to dole out discipline, they always came back and thanked me. They knew they had done wrong and they knew I had treated them with love and tenderness and caring and professionalism, as well as holding them to task. I never judged them. I said, this act is bad. You're not bad. I value you so much, but we're going to deal with this."

Katherine remembered one incident early in her tenure as an incident commander that tested her leadership skills. "It was my first fire when I was an acting chief. There was a captain that everyone on the department was scared of. We all responded to a fire, and this house was raging, but the captain would not get out of the truck, and he wouldn't let his crew get off the truck. A firefighter inside the building fell through the floor, and I did not have a RIT (Rapid Intervention Team) on the scene because this guy would not get off the truck. He told his guys to sit back and watch. It was because I was in charge."

"It was around two in the morning. The next day I started my own investigation of what had happened. I had a good friend who was on his truck company and he told me, Katherine, he wouldn't let us get off the truck. We started to get off and he told us, shut the door and sit down. We're going to wait and see what happens. It was the first time that captain had ever done anything like that."

"So I went to my chief with what I had learned, and I told him I wanted to follow up. I asked my chief to come with me when I confronted this captain. He told me he didn't want to, and that I could do it by myself. This was the scariest officer on the entire department. Even the chiefs were intimidated by him. So I went and talked to the captain, and he started raking me over the coals. He was telling me everything I did wrong at the fire. And I said, I know I made mistakes—read my report. It was my first fire as a chief!"

"I handed him the disciplinary letter and made him sign it. I had cleared it with the department lawyer. The letter said, if you ever do anything that could be construed as jeopardizing firefighter safety again, you will be terminated. When I left there, I was shaking like a leaf. I would not back down. No matter what the captain said to me, I kept telling him, this is not about me. This is about you. And my chief, who did not support me with this and never really liked me, said to me afterward, well Katherine, you just might make one hell of a battalion chief after all."

"The next time I was acting chief was about a month later, and I went to this captain's station. I walked into the station and gave the usual greetings and information. Then as I was leaving, this captain said, Katherine, come here. And he gave me a big hug and said, I just want to tell you that I am so sorry. And from that day forward, that man called me and emailed up until around two years after he retired to make sure I was doing okay and that no one was messing with me."

Katherine spent many years as an active member and board president of the national organization Women in the Fire Service. "Being the voice of women firefighters was kind of a heavy burden at times. But the tremendous opportunities it brought were the biggest blessing I ever had in the fire service."

"I don't have a lot of pain from my fire service career, but I do have some, from being one of the first women to do this job. But what is so awesome is to see these younger women who don't have that. They don't have the same history. It's not because they're in denial. There are some women who are just truly excelling and doing phenomenal work in the fire service. It's humbling to know that I may have helped to make that happen."

Patricia Dyas

Patricia Dyas in her office

# Tenacity

Patricia Dyas had already graduated from college and served in the U.S. Marine Corps when she took the test for firefighter in Shreveport, Louisiana. "I was at the maximum age limit of 28 at that time. I was waiting for a position in my field of recreation therapy to open up at the VA Hospital and was taking civil service exams so I could work until that other position opened up. The fire department happened to be one of them." She laughed. "I thought I'd just work until that position opened up." That was in 1981. Now Pat Dyas is the Chief of Prevention for the Shreveport Fire Department.

It has not been an easy road. Pat was among three women who were the first to be hired by the department. The fire department had been under a consent decree for discriminatory hiring since 1974. "It was very difficult. I was targeted to prove that the fire department was not a place for women, and that we couldn't do the job. I looked very young for my age, so a lot of the guys thought I was much younger than I was. They did not know I had gone to college, that I had a degree, that I had been in the United States Marine Corps. They didn't know anything about me. They didn't even know how old I was. They were just determined to prove this was not a place for a woman. And I was the one they decided to prove that on."

As a result, Pat was sent to every fire station "so they could work on me. Fortunately I was an educated person. I had a college degree, and had started working on my fire science degree. But I was having to defend myself on paper all the time. So I read—the administrative procedures, operations standards. I knew the rules, and they were violating their own policies. I was not afraid to defend myself."

Those early years were tough. "Guys were doing all kinds of crazy stuff. They tried to make me hoist this ladder. But I told them, when I went through training, it took three of us to raise this, and you want me to do this by myself? So my position to my captain was, if I get injured doing a procedure you shouldn't make me do, I will sue you. There were a lot of little things going on all the time—racial stuff, sexual stuff. Each time I had to let them know—not me."

"At drills they would try to embarrass me. So I said, okay, I can do some things you think I can't do. And I would do it. I had just got out of the Marine Corps, so I was physically fit to do a lot of stuff they didn't think I could do, and do it by myself. A lot of things they wanted me to do by myself when I knew from basic training that normally you had more than one person do it."

"When the department went into the EMS service, it was supposed to be strictly on a volunteer basis. But I was assigned to the medic unit. So I talked to the district chief about it and said, this letter says strictly volunteer. The chief said, that's a woman's job, you should be doing that. I had to explain, that's not a woman's job, that's a position where you volunteer to do it. I had to write a letter saying I did not want to be assigned to that unit. And they did end up taking me off."

After five years on the line, Pat took the exam for fire inspector. The test resulted in three people on the list for the position. When the other two candidates dropped off the list, "the department tried to call for another test because they didn't want me in fire prevention. But the civil service law at that time said you could not call for another test until you exhausted the list. So once again I had to call the district chief and explain what the civil service law said."

"I went to work up there, and the deputy chief told the guys he couldn't stand the idea of calling a nigger woman a captain." All inspectors in the fire prevention bureau held the rank of captain at that time. "So he wrote a memo saying from now on none of the people in fire prevention would be captains. They had to take off their name tags, take their badges off, and they couldn't pass out any more business cards. The guys wanted me to file a lawsuit. But I said, hey, I just got here. I don't care if nobody calls me captain. So the others got together and signed a letter, and the order was rescinded."

Even after thirty years, Pat describes work as a constant challenge but has persevered largely due to her faith. "God has a purpose for each and every one of us. I feel it was God's purpose for me to fill this position and make a way for women behind me, and to let people know a woman can do this job and do it well, and persevere through everything you can throw at her. When these other women see me, they have all the respect in the world for me because they know I've had some challenges, but I'm still walking around here, I'm still proud, and I'm still sticking with it."

"What has made me proud since I have joined the fire department is the response I get from people I meet in my community. People I don't even remember from my childhood come up to me and tell me,

I knew you were going to do something great. I'm so proud of you. And just to make it through retirement—these other ladies, they look at me and say, she's doing it. She's sticking with it. So I'm going to stick with it too."

"I've always fought for what's right. We have a thing on the fire department about being a team player. I'll be a team player when you're right and fair. But if you're wrong, I am not a team player. These ladies see me and say, she's fought, she's stood up for what's right, she's going to be fair, and she's still here and her head is still high. She's still smiling, and she's still making history. That is my legacy."

Tamala Wilson

Tamala "Spanky" Wilson in her district

## Forgiveness

Tamala "Spanky" Wilson joined the Durham, North Carolina Fire
Department in 1990. She promoted up through the ranks until 2009
when she was made a battalion chief. Prior to becoming a firefighter,
Spanky was a high school physical education teacher and coach.

Being a firefighter hasn't always been easy. "When I made relief
driver early in my career, I was transferred to another shift with an
acting captain whose best friend was the rookie firefighter on the
truck with me. The two of them were partners in crime. It was a
totally hostile environment for me there. I was driving the truck in an

acting position, the officer was acting in his captain's position, and our captain was the acting battalion chief."

Tamala's new co-workers set the tone early. "There was another woman on the department who would speak up about problems, and they would say about her, 'She just needs a good hard fuck.' They would try to set me up to fail in as many situations as they could. They were so mean spirited and bullying that I tried to stay away from them as much as I could—I would be in the kitchen if they were in the apparatus bay, for example. Then they would say, Let's go clean tiles and not tell her about it, then we can write her up for not participating. Things like that."

"When I read my acting captain's logs for my evaluation, I was shocked, because all these things were on there and I didn't have a clue that I hadn't participated in them. It was written in such a way to try to get rid of me. Then one day I was at home, and I got an anonymous email picture. It was really disgusting and pornographic. I suspected one of my coworkers had sent it, but I couldn't prove it. So I got a computer expert to come to my house, and they identified this acting captain as the one who sent it. When I went to work the next day, I confronted him and told him I had proof he did it. And he said, oh, I was just kidding, can't you take a joke?"

"It was a really difficult and hostile environment and I had to fight it all by myself. At that point, when he sent that picture to me, I went to the acting battalion chief. I told him, I can't work in this environment anymore. These guys hate me and I'm afraid if we're in a fire they might leave me or do something terrible. And the battalion chief told me, Oh no, they're good guys, they've just never worked with a woman firefighter before. They just need time to adapt. And I said, what's so different about me compared to anyone else they work with? Why can't they treat me with the respect they would a brother? But the battalion chief didn't do anything about it. He just let it go."

"I decided I had a choice. I certainly had enough ammunition that I could have won a sexual harassment case against the fire department. But I weighed it against how much I loved everything else about the job. It was a busy station with lots of fires, so I got a lot of experience. To me, going into structure fires and putting them out was an indescribable high. I didn't want to give that up. I knew if I pursued the sexual harassment complaint, I could be ostracized by other people I could prove myself to. They wouldn't give me a chance if they thought I just wanted to make trouble."

"So I made a decision I was going to stay and work really hard and prove myself. It wasn't the whole department, it was just these two jerks. If I thought it was system wide, I probably would have taken it to the next level. But from what I had seen, it was just these two guys. So I decided I would try to make myself the best I could be, and get out of there as soon as I could."

"I was inspired at that point. I got my two-year degree, I took every kind of class I could, I got certified in everything. I became a member of the new tactical rescue team. Then I made permanent driver, and was sent to another shift. And things really started moving in a positive direction at that point."

"Five years later, I was a brand new captain. The guy who had been my acting captain during the bad times worked on his off days cutting trees. And that day he had gotten into a bunch of bees. A 911 call went out, and we responded. I saw him on the ground there paralyzed. His eyes were open, but he was barely breathing and was near death. We treated him and gave him epinephrine right away, and got him into the ambulance. The paramedics had to intubate him on the way to the hospital, and he almost died twice en route."

"We followed the ambulance, and when we got to the hospital, I stayed with him all day. I just felt that no matter how bad he was to me, he was still part of my family. We needed to do everything we could for him. And that experience seemed to totally turn him around. He sent us a letter telling us how appreciative he was and how much he loved us, and that he saw us as part of his family. And he and I have had a good relationship since then."

"He is a changed person. He was young and immature, and that was the thing to do among a few of the guys—harass the new women on the job. Just like everyone else who was more open minded from the get-go, he had to go through exposure to women doing the job every day and seeing they could do it, and develop that respect that he already had for the guys. And now he knows. It took him a long time. He's very respectful to me now. And he is still a driver, and I am a battalion chief."

"There have been several times that I have been this man's boss. I didn't treat him any differently. A lot of people who know what happened between us asked me, how could you stay at the hospital with him all day? Why did you go above and beyond? And I tell them, because he's my brother. They don't necessarily have to feel it about you for you to want to reciprocate. That's the way I felt—that this is my family, and these are my brothers and sisters, and I need to do everything I can for them."

"In the end, it wasn't just me who changed things. It was all the women on the job. I believe that's the way to change things—just creating that exposure, so they work with us every day and they see we can do the job. Then there is no respect problem anymore."

"I am most proud of being able to help people in all walks of life in many different ways. I feel a sense of pride and accomplishment that I can make a difference on a regular basis, and we get feedback on what we do right away."

"As far as legacy, as a supervisor I'm trying to change some of the old school methods of just do as I say, with lots of ego involved, intimidation and scare tactics. I've tried to change that by putting people first, and considering them in how I manage, and it is much more effective. My people appreciate my style of leadership a lot more than what they were used to. I'm trying to change the fire service in my own immediate surroundings toward an environment where people can work together without fear."

# Chapter 8

## Animal Tales

A fundamental cliché about firefighters is that they rescue cats in trees. They have those big ladders, so why not? In fact, few fire departments still do so, the risk of injury to firefighters outweighing any benefit to the animals. And as firefighters like to point out, how many cat skeletons have you ever seen in trees?

Still, firefighters have plenty of animal contacts in their working lives. Pets, livestock, and assistance animals are victims of fires and accidents the same as their owners are. Many people will refuse to leave a burning building without their pets, and window stickers are available now that tell firefighters how many animals are in a structure and where they are located. It is unknown which firefighter originally attempted CPR on a dog or cat after a fire, but now it is standard practice to attempt to resuscitate animals, and many fire departments carry specialized gear for this purpose.

Beyond fires and accidents, firefighters encounter animals in many other ways in their jobs. Firefighters are generalists by nature, and they have a lot of different types of equipment and tools, so if someone else can't help with the problem… well, who are you going to call?

As a result, firefighters fish dogs from frozen lakes, extricate pet rabbits from pipes, and corral squirrels that have invaded homes. I have personally responded to "a cockatoo and person stuck in a tree" (a sheepish looking person twenty feet up a tree, and a smug looking bird about ten feet above him) and a midnight call for a raccoon that fell down a chimney behind a woodstove (thankfully not burning at the time.) The raccoon was stunned but not injured, and once it came to its senses, it was plenty mad. It took three firefighters, a police officer, and an animal control officer over an hour to finally pull it to safety.

On my department, a fire crew was called when a bear was treed in a neighborhood and when a champion steer got loose from a stock show parade downtown. Two firefighters I worked with then liked to spend free time in the evenings at the station practicing roping on a hay bale with horns on it. They were very excited about this last call, imagining that they might get some real roping experience. Happily for the steer and for them, their expertise was not needed.

Firefighters do not only encounter animals as victims needing help but also as coworkers dedicated to a common mission. Wilderness and urban search and rescue dogs lead emergency responders to trapped victims, and over a hundred dogs worked at the World Trade Center in the aftermath of 9/11. Dogs are certified to detect accelerants and explosives, and help discover the point of origin and cause of fires. Dogs and other animals are increasingly included as members of crisis response teams to aid victims of disasters, crimes, and other trauma.

In the old days, dalmatians were often part of fire crews, with the specific function of clearing intersections for the horse-drawn fire pumps, as well as guarding the horses at the scene. Dalmatians are the pet of choice for many firefighters, due to their distinctive look and place in the history of the fire service. Some fire companies still own a dalmatian or other station dog.

Firefighters exist to serve their communities, and all communities include animals, either as pets, livestock, or working animals. As firefighters constantly improve skills and equipment to better meet the needs of the human members of their communities, so must they consider how to serve and protect the non-human creatures for which they are also responsible.

Nicol Juratovac and her crew after a successful dog rescue

Nicol Juratovac

# Specialty Station

Nicol Juratovac decided to become a firefighter in 1992, but making that dream come true took a little time. She took the test for the San Francisco Fire Department that year, but the fact she did not pass it only reinforced her commitment to do better the next time around. As she waited for the next test opportunity to come up, Nicol went to law school and worked part-time as a limo driver and a bicycle messenger in the city.

In 1997, right after she graduated from law school and was preparing for the bar exam, the San Francisco Fire Department held another hiring test. She took the test, did well, was offered the firefighter's position, and never looked back. "A lot of people in my family wanted me to take the bar exam, but I said, forget that. I just got the greatest job in the world."

In 2000, Nicol promoted to lieutenant, and in 2010, as an acting captain, was assigned to Station 19 on the west side of the city, one of San Francisco's surf rescue stations. Her station also specializes in cliff rescue and handles many auto extrications as well as residential and high rise fires. "We do it all. In order to make this house, you have to be surf rescue qualified, which means you have to swim 400 yards in under ten minutes in a pool. That's just the first component on Day One." The first day of the test also includes doing multiple surface dives, treading water for extended periods, and other endurance activities.

"After the swimming pool they throw you out there in the Pacific Ocean and have you do simulated rescues. Then they take you out on the fire boat to the middle of the bay and throw you in the water and you have to swim in open water back to shore in less than ten minutes." Nicol practiced for six months before taking the grueling test. "It was such a struggle, but now I love it." Nicol commented that the fact everyone at the station must pass this test creates a real *esprit de corps* among all firefighters at the station. "This is really an arena where women can definitely be as good as the guys."

Another specialty of Station 19 is cliff rescue, and those rescued are as often canine as human. The station borders Fort Funston, a unit of the National Park Service that features 200-300 foot cliffs overlooking the ocean. "It's one of the most scenic areas in the city. Many people walk their dogs here, on trails that are right along the cliff edge." Sometimes unleashed dogs just slip over the edge, or sometimes, "the dogs are running, running, running and they just run right off the edge of the cliff."

"What's really funny about San Francisco is that there are more registered pets than there are children. It's a singles kind of place, and too expensive for families here. We joke around that whenever we have a person over the side of the cliff, people just walk on by like it's no big deal. But when they find out there's a dog over there, oh my goodness. They all hang out on the edge of the cliff and it's a real chore to get them away from the area. They're all taking photographs and before we even get back to the firehouse, it's on YouTube."

Nicol's first dog rescue of many came in her first week at Station 19. She acted as safety officer for an operation that involved an engine, a truck, and the battalion chief. As they fixed an anchor on the battalion chief's truck, one firefighter was belayed down to the dog. The station has an abundance of technical rescue equipment, but "one thing we don't have is a dog harness. With this dog, the firefighter had to literally carry him back up the rock face." Nicol commented, "Most of the dogs have been very cooperative. They don't bite—they're just like, get me the hell out of here!" This dog expressed his gratitude after being rescued by jumping up and licking the face of the person who rescued him.

In 2011, Nicol tested for the permanent captain's position, hoping to maintain her current role as truck company officer at Station 19, at least in the near future. She appreciates the "mental gymnastics" that go with truck operations. "You're constantly thinking. Where can we throw the 35 foot ladder? Should I split the crew? Should I go to the roof? What about search and rescue? How do we gain entry for the engine? I'm very lucky to have these young guys and girls on my crew now who are very aggressive and who have spent most of their careers on the truck. They're teaching me some things."

"It's been a humbling experience to be here. The crew has given me the chance to succeed. As an officer, I'm more of a coach. It's worked out really well. I've never felt more comfortable."

Krista Wyatt

Krista Wyatt and the rescued deer

# The Abandoned Deer

Although Krista Wyatt has done other jobs, as a school teacher and a town recreation director, being a firefighter is what she was meant to do. Currently a captain with the Lebanon, Ohio Fire Department where she has been a member since 1986, Krista is also chief of the Carlisle, Ohio Volunteer Fire Department, a position she has held since 2009. "I fall into that category where I'm always a firefighter. I have to check emergency lights in hotel hallways and sit in restaurants facing the exit. It never leaves me. I've never had another job do that to me." Still, Krista finds time to enjoy her other passion—motorcycles. "I started a business working on motorcycles before I took the Carlisle job. I ride as much as I can."

Over the years, Krista has had the opportunity to help many non-human members of her community. "I've rescued cats, dogs, birds, horses, removed bats from houses. I always get tapped to remove pet snakes from their cages when we have fires, and it is so funny to watch men run from me when I do that! People's pets are important."

One of Krista's most memorable animal rescues involved a fawn that had been abandoned by its mother. When it was clear that the mother was not returning for its baby, someone called the fire department for help. The fawn was hungry and weak. "One of our medics had goats so she suggested I scoop up the fawn and cradle her while she tried to feed her with the bottle. As you can probably imagine, I wore a lot of the food, but we managed to get enough in her. One of the police officers has a sister who runs an animal refuge place so they came to pick her up and as far as I know she still lives freely there. I have to say helping that fawn was much neater than most things I've done."

"I'm proud that I've had a positive impact on people's lives. Whether it is seeing someone walk down the street that we saved with CPR or seeing a firefighter doing a good job after being that person's instructor, I get to see the difference I have made in my little corner of the world."

"I'm extremely proud of what I've been able to do as the chief of a volunteer department that was in decline. I hope my legacy will be that I did this job because I truly cared about people and the communities I served. When they look back on what I have done, I hope they say I did my job well and had a great time doing it."

Karen Simpson

Karen Simpson on water patrol

# The Great Chase

Karen Simpson has been a firefighter with the Chatham-Kent, Ontario Fire Department since 2005. The fire district is located around fifty miles outside of Detroit and has three full time stations as well as sixteen volunteer stations. As a first class firefighter, she rotates as a driver and firefighter on all the department's vehicles. Before becoming a firefighter, Karen was a personal trainer and also worked in marketing for a company that handled sports entertainment.

Firefighters are known as being jacks-of-all-trades, and recently Karen and her crew took on a new role. "We were out at the end of a shift running errands like getting fuel and dropping off laundry. I was driving, and as we were going down the road, I could see that traffic was backed up. We'd just had a bad storm and I thought maybe it was black ice that the drivers were slowing down for. As we drove a short distance, I saw what appeared to be a dog in the middle of the road."

"I thought, this isn't good. It was a four-lane highway and the dog was running down the centerline. As we got closer, I could see that the dog was a purebred boxer, maybe someone's $800 pet. I told my captain what I saw, since he couldn't see it from the other side of the rig. He called the OSPCA, the provincial animal control agency. I asked the captain, what do you think we should do? And he said he thought we should just keep following it."

"We were approaching some pretty big intersections and we thought this dog would certainly cause an accident. Sure enough, several cars hit the brakes, went up on the curb, a couple near misses. So we turned our overhead lights on, not only so people would see us, but also that they would pull over and give this dog a little more space."

"My captain had never been in this situation before and wasn't exactly sure what to do. It wasn't a critical call, but we were in an area where there could be some major wrecks because of what was going on. He got on the radio and told dispatch, we're still following this dog, and it seems to be approaching Walmart. So dispatch asked, is it turning into Walmart? But the dog had run past, so my captain said, no, it does not appear that he is going shopping... The dog ran up to the next intersection and the captain said, he's turning left, bypassing the Home Depot... So we're having this commentary with dispatch and I don't know if they thought we were serious or not. But it was really funny to hear the captain giving a play-by-play of this dog running through the streets."

"After a few more intersections, we were outside of our district. We radioed for the other main station in Chatham to cover the calls until this was over. Finally when we had clear roads, I accelerated and pulled the truck in at a 45-degree angle. The whole crew piled off the truck to try to nab the dog on the shoulder of the road. And we finally got him. His paws were bloodied, and his tag indicated he lived over an hour away. The next day I drove the same route, and realized that this dog had run in a full sprint for over five kilometers."

"We called the owners and told them we had their dog in our firetruck. And they were thrilled, so it had a happy ending. Even though we normally don't rescue cats from trees or chase lost dogs, we definitely prevented a few collisions that day."

"The thing I am most proud of is being able to do good things in my community. It's a privilege. I was hired with that trust in mind. It is a really good feeling to make a positive difference for someone who is having the worst day of their life."

"As far as legacy, I did not choose some of what I will leave behind. I just wanted to be a firefighter. But about a year and a half after I was hired, I was the plaintiff in a huge harassment and discrimination investigation that led to a shift in our culture. It hasn't been easy. A lot of people associate me with what happened and there might be connections I never get with certain firefighters because of it. But the bad behavior—the bullying and teasing and harassment—it's happening less and less, and I don't think it will ever happen with me. I feel like I've drawn a line as to how I can be treated."

"I feel I have been a big part of the shift in our culture. Now I coach other firefighters on the subject of bullying and speak in schools. I wouldn't wish this experience on anybody, but it has led to changes in our culture that were really necessary. It wasn't pleasant and it probably took years off my life. But I wouldn't change any of it, because what I did really made a difference, and it made it better for women and others who come in after me."

Beth Heim

Beth Heim at the fire station

## The Smallest Survivor

Firefighting is a family tradition for Beth Heim. Since 2000, she has been a member of the Liberty Hose Company, an all-volunteer fire department that serves the town of Williamstown, Pennsylvania around 45 minutes north of the state capital Harrisburg. In addition, her sister, father, grandfather, and great-grandfather have also been volunteers with the same organization. Beth's stepdaughter is now considering joining the department as well. Beth is currently a chief engineer and training coordinator for the department. She also works as an EMT with the Dalmatia Ambulance Company. "I can't get away from it," Beth said. "It's my whole life."

Beth remembered a fire in a duplex in 2009 that had unexpected consequences. "The call came in that someone was trapped. As we arrived on scene we called the dispatcher and were told to stand down because the person entrapped had a gun. We didn't know exactly what to do at that point. Electrical wires were popping off the house and sparking in the street. Then we heard a gun shot."

"My assistant chief ran to the side of the house where the fire started and looked through the window. He saw a man lying on the floor. We went into action to try to put the fire out and get to him. But the man inside had barricaded the door. By the time we could get access to that half of the house, the other half had ignited. The entire duplex and the house beside it were now engulfed in flames. It took us about an hour to put it out. We had fire companies on all sides of the structures dumping water on it."

"The fire was mostly out when my team went into the other half of the house. We were checking for hot spots and making sure we didn't miss anything. We went upstairs and were getting ready to break through the wall to get to the other side, to check for fire over there. We had to gain access this way because the stairs on the other side had completely burned through."

"My partner was getting ready to fire up the chain saw and I heard something, so I told him to stop. We heard a whimpering sound. I got down on my hands and knees and was crawling toward the sound, and there was this kitten behind the refrigerator. I couldn't believe it survived. It was so small it fit in my hand. Her nose and ears were burned, as well as the hair on her back. But the refrigerator saved her."

"Because of that fire, I ended up finding that kitten, and now I'm a member of PASART, the Pennsylvania State Animal Response Team. The team is made up of volunteers that range from firefighters and EMTs to veterinarians and doctors. In the event of a disaster like a flood, we go out to residences where homeowners had to leave and could not take their pets. We search for the animals, rescue them, and return them to their owners. We also help free trapped animals, like a horse that fell down some basement steps and broke its legs."

"Being part of PASART allows me to help animals in their time of need when they are the last thing on others' minds. Animals are people too."

Lynette Jelinek

Lynette Jelinek and Topaz

# Fire Dogs

Lynette Jelinek is not a firefighter, but her partner Topaz is. Topaz, a three year old Labrador Retriever, is a sworn, badge-carrying member of the Glendale, Arizona Fire Department's Crisis Response Team.

Lynette was a volunteer with the Peoria, Arizona Fire Department in 2002 when her next door neighbor, a captain with the Glendale Fire Department, asked her to consider putting together a program that would provide support for citizens and firefighters during and after emergencies. Lynette had a background in psychology but at that time was working in a family business that managed fuel delivery from bulk plants. Initially, Lynette worked alone as a volunteer building the program and then was paid on a contract basis, but within a few years, the program had four full time employees, as well as dozens of volunteers.

The program is staffed 24 hours every day out of one of Glendale's fire stations, and provides services for families, victims, and witnesses after a significant emergency event. "We basically put our firefighters back into service. We are trained to deal with domestic violence, homicides, suicides, drownings, codes, and provide emotional support and follow up for those who are affected. We're like a mini-Red Cross—we have clothes and shoes and baby formula and a whole library of resources for people in crisis situations."

Topaz joined the department in 2008. Originally trained by the Michigan organization Paws with a Cause, Topaz was on track to become a seizure response dog, but "we career-changed him. He goes on calls like car accidents, or calls that involve children or just people who like animals. He's there to help get the victim's mind off what happened or simply calm people down."

The team has found that Topaz can accomplish things that no human members of the fire department are capable of. "We went on a car accident because the battalion chief wanted help with handling a little girl in a car seat. The child's grandmother had been driving and had hit a pedestrian. The little girl didn't seem to be hurt, but was scared to death. The firefighters on the scene had pretty much cleared her for injuries but wanted to get her out of the car seat. But every time they would touch the car seat, she would scream and go crazy. She wouldn't let anyone near her, even other members of the crisis team that were already on the scene, and she wouldn't respond to any questions."

"So I walked over and said, 'Hey, I have a dog in my car who would really like to meet you.' And she stopped screaming. I asked her, 'Do you like dogs?' and she shook her head yes. I said, 'I need to know what your name is.' And she said, 'My name is Crystal: C-R-Y-S-T-A-L.' And I was able to talk to her and determine that she was not hurt.

Then I went over to get the dog and quickly got her out of the vehicle."

"That was solid gold to me. Topaz can do in three seconds what it can take twenty minutes to do in any other situation. We had her out of the car seat, throwing the ball for the dog, talking. That's what our work is about—getting people to disassociate with what is going on otherwise and establishing that relationship and communication with people in crisis."

On another call, a high school student drowned in a pool in front of many of his classmates. "Normally it is really hard to relate to high school students in crisis. They're too cool, and they don't want to listen. But we were able to take Topaz in and get them to open up on a whole different level. With the dog, we always have people's undivided attention."

Although Topaz lives with Lynette and her family, she does not own him. He's a member of the fire department, and the fact he has a badge means that he is protected the same as any other firefighter while doing emergency response. "We do go on some pretty ugly calls sometimes. If someone were to assault him at a scene, because he is a sworn peace dog that act would be a felony rather than a misdemeanor." Topaz is currently the only crisis support dog on the Glendale Fire Department, but Lynette has been asked by the fire chief to consider adding others. "I'm looking forward to making this program bigger and providing support for a very long time."

# Chapter 9

## Acquainted with the Night

No one knows the night like emergency responders. Others might be awake, working a night shift at a factory or getting up to care for a sick child. But emergency responders are out in the world at night, calling on people at their homes, driving the streets, hiking the ridges and canyons, watching the quiet dramas of the shadows. Sometimes just sitting around, waiting. Firefighters may sleep, but it is in narrow beds in dormitories or sleeping bags on the ground, places very unlike their own homes. And sleep is often disrupted by the snoring coworker or the anxiety of a new officer who is anticipating the first big fire.

Most firefighters work 24 hour shifts, and sometimes as many as 48 hours at a stretch. On a wildland fire, days on the fireline often become weeks, and sleep is something you do when you can. A busy night is exhausting—if you're lucky, there might be a nap in a chair or in the cab of a truck. But being awake at night in the city, or driving the country roads, or standing watch on the forest fireline is also thrilling and beautiful in its own way, and some of my most vivid memories are from the night calls.

Everything at night is stranger, funnier, more intense. The fires seem bigger and the medical calls more sinister or sad. The worst things seem to happen in the middle of the night, like the movie theater manager who was murdered directly across from the fire station, or the baby discovered by her father dead in her crib from SIDS. One night we encountered a carefree woman first at midnight, when one of the guys she was partying with broke his ankle. A couple hours later in the trailer of a different guy, we found the same woman beaten nearly to death. Suicide attempts often happen at night, and one shift at around two in the morning, my crew responded to a young man who had cut himself multiple times with a razor. When we entered the apartment, there were pools of blood on the floor and the receiver of the phone had a dripping bloody handprint on it, like something from a horror movie.

One of the biggest windstorms in Boulder's history hit one night when I had two years on the job. Boulder is famous for its winter Chinooks—dry, sustained hurricane force winds that can last over twelve hours. The wind was howling by the time we went to bed that night, and we slept fitfully until the moment we were all awakened by a blinding blue flash, as every transformer in North Boulder exploded at once. I remember jolting awake and hearing one of the guys say quietly, "Uh oh."

Then it began, as we responded to hundreds of wind-related emergency calls around the city. Large Dumpsters were blown down streets into cars and sheets of construction plywood flew around like cards. At one point, we were staged next to a three story building where the roof was peeling off. The wind suddenly shifted and large chunks of roofing came straight for our engine. In a mad scramble we saved ourselves, but all three of the ladders mounted on the side of the engine were destroyed.

When I was an officer, my engine was called one winter night for standby on a hostage situation that was taking place in a residential neighborhood. We were required to simply wait in the vehicle until called by the police, but the incident went on for hours, and we never were called. We were not supposed to run the engine, as the police did not want to draw attention to the scene. So we sat, shivering and bundled up in our bunker gear, wearing our headsets more for warmth than communication.

Then somehow it started—the engineer and I started singing every song we knew, sometimes in harmony and sometimes separately. Our high-tech headsets with microphones made our voices sound much better than they normally would. In this way, we kept ourselves going through a cold and uncomfortable night. The firefighter, separated from us in the rear seat, could hardly believe his ears, especially since the engineer on this incident was one of the toughest and scariest on the job. The next morning, when the firefighter said something about what had happened the night before, the engineer and I both categorically denied it.

I remember the beauty of night on the job—the absolute quiet of the snowbound streets at three in the morning on Christmas Day, the rare display of the Northern Lights over a routine accident scene. After an all-night fire, when you are dirty, exhausted, and soaked with sweat, there is nothing so welcome or sublime as the first rays of sun breaking through the morning haze, the sky lightening from black to gray to blue. The experience of it was simple and complete: I am a firefighter, and this is another day.

Joette Borzik

Joette Borzik at the Yellowstone Fires of 1988

# Spike Camp

Joette Borzik knew from a young age that she wanted to work in natural resource management, which led her to pursue a degree in forestry from Pennsylvania State University. But she "didn't necessarily know I would find a career in wildland fire. I just kind of fell into it. But I really enjoyed it, because it was so adventurous. I'm an adventure seeker."

Joette began her Forest Service career as a seasonal employee in 1980, while still in college. She graduated from Penn State in 1981 and moved into fire related work in 1983 with the U.S. Forest Service. Initially working as a forestry technician, her career became focused entirely on fire management in 1983, and she continued to work in wildland fire operations through 2005. She left the Forest Service and began work with the U.S. Fish and Wildlife Service in 1996, and in 1998 became a fire training specialist for the National Interagency Fire Center in Boise, Idaho. Joette retired in 2011 and is now pursuing a second career with her training and consulting company Growth Journey.

Joette described her initial career path. "I started out at the bottom as a firefighter and moved up to squad boss and crew boss. Then strike team leader and division group supervisor. When I wasn't on wildland fire, I was working on prescribed fire. That took care of our time in the off season. Then during the fire season, everyone went to suppression."

Wildland firefighters must frequently camp out along the fireline. "For a wildland firefighter, staying out overnight is not a big deal. You're there until the fire is out. I can't tell you how many nights I've spent sleeping outdoors, on the fireline or elsewhere. I don't know how many wildland fires I have fought. I do remember during the summer of 1985 as a Redmond (Oregon) Hotshot firefighter, we fought 65 wildland fires just that summer."

Although most wildland fires are extinguished when small, many require camps that are established for days or weeks at a time. "We call it Spike Camp when you're out there and it's too far to come back at night. So we set up a camp, and somebody delivers food to you. If you're in a remote area, it's usually helicoptered in to you." Firefighters often work for sixteen hour shifts, taking rest breaks when they can. Firefighters working at such camps must carry their own gear, usually lightweight space blankets for shelter.

In 1987, Joette worked on the Silver Fire in the Kalmiopsis Wilderness Area of southern Oregon and northern California. The fire eventually charred 150,000 acres and required her to stay in fire camp for over two months. "It was steep and rugged terrain, very beautiful, but the fire was huge. I was a division group supervisor, assigned in a very remote area. Once we got people there, we kept them there, as it just wasn't feasible to bring them back and forth."

"The fire caused a severe smoke inversion in the area that persisted for months. The outside air was so hard to breathe at times that oxygen tents were brought into fire camp for firefighters to use as needed. I can remember being in my sleeping bag one night, trying to sleep, and the smoke was so bad that I pulled my head into the sleeping bag so I wouldn't have to smell the smoke."

"At times there was really no place to totally get out of the smoke. The fireline had smoke on it, the fire camp had smoke in it, and the community was evacuated because there was fire and smoke in it. But somebody had to extinguish the fire, and you couldn't fight a wildland fire in a respirator."

Even under such difficult conditions, Joette remembered some transcendent moments during her time on the Silver Fire. "Food came by helicopter, cans of food delivered in cardboard boxes. It came in a big net and everybody would be really excited when the helicopter came because they knew it was chow time. We set up a buffet line of cardboard boxes at the helispot, with people serving the food from different cans."

"So there were all these cardboard boxes in the area. We had a number of Native American fire crews working at that camp, and one night they took the cardboard boxes and started drumming on them. One drummer started and then people started joining in, and it became a small gathering on the mountain top overlooking this beautiful area. They began to sing and chant, and honor their American Indian culture, banging on the cardboard boxes from our food that night. It was such a spiritual feeling that I was overcome with. We were one with the earth and with the universe. It was a very special moment."

"In wildand firefighting there was sometimes rivalry between the Native American crews, who were often from different tribes. But none of that mattered when everyone was sitting together on that mountain top, and we all had a common purpose and mission. We were there together all alone, and it was very quiet. All you could hear was the chanting and the drumming. It was wonderful. I think of it now and I get chills."

Joette has some concerns about the future of wildland firefighting. "I think it's a profession that appeals to a unique individual and not everybody is adventurous and wants to be in the outdoors. Not everybody wants to do hard work. I think it's going to be harder to recruit women and men to these kinds of professions in the future, when you look at how people spend less and less time outdoors."

"There are a number of books written recently about nature deficit syndrome with children. Many children are afraid of the outdoors and their parents are afraid to let them be outdoors and to get dirty. Well, natural resource and wildland fire careers have the basic premise that you are comfortable being outdoors and don't mind getting dirty. A lot of kids don't want to be in the woods or to exercise. The obesity rates in children are pretty high these days, and those are our future wildland and structural firefighters. Unless something changes, we could have trouble recruiting firefighters in the future."

"When I was growing up, I was in the woods, down at the creek, picking out crayfish from the pond, playing in the mud. I was coming back at the end of the day thinking about how I had seen ten different tree species out there. I just wanted it more and more. I was so comfortable being out there, but I don't see it so much anymore."

Brenda Berkman

Brenda Berkman after a night fire

# Night in the City

Brenda Berkman was an attorney practicing employment and immigration law in New York City when she took the test to become a firefighter in 1978. "A lot of people thought I was completely nuts. But my parents had always pushed civil service jobs. At one point I had thought of going into the military. I was raised to believe you should be of service to your community. It was a significant part of my growing up."

Brenda thought about becoming a police officer when she first moved to New York City, but did not feel she had the temperament for law enforcement. "My ex-husband had represented the fire officers' union with his law firm, and I had met a lot of fire officers through him. And I sat next to a guy in law school who was a complete fire buff." Brenda talked to a lot of people about her potential interest in the fire service, and in 1977, her next-door neighbor told her that the department would be testing. She put in her application within two days of the filing deadline.

The FDNY had never hired a woman as a firefighter, and no woman had ever passed the department's physical test. The test Brenda took in 1978, the first open to women, was widely recognized as the hardest test ever given by the department. When no women passed the test despite extensive training and preparation, Brenda filed a lawsuit with the city that eventually led to the first women being hired with the FDNY in 1982. Brenda was among that first group, and she served on the department until her retirement in 2006 as a captain. Brenda worked at the World Trade Center on 9/11 and continues to work as a volunteer at the Tribute World Trade Center Visitors Center, which was established by the 9/11 Families Association.

Some of Brenda's strong memories from the job relate to experiences of night in the city. "I liked being awake in the city at night. It was fantastic. Some streets always had traffic on them, but side streets and commercial areas would be completely deserted except for maybe some prostitutes or illegal late nightclubs. I loved the idea that we were up and about and going into these areas of the city when everyone else was asleep, and had no idea what was going on out there. They'd have no clue until the next morning when they got up and turned on their televisions of the wild and crazy things that happened in the city overnight."

"This city is so huge, with so many different people from all over the world. We got to see everything. It was a really interesting and fun part of the job. But it was also important work, because we were the ones that people called as their last resort, no matter what their problem was."

Night also brought danger. "At the beginning of my career, I never had problems sleeping at the fire station, even with people snoring and all that. I was good about being able to relax on night tours. But I attribute that to the fact I really didn't know very much then. Later on when I learned more things, and was responsible for people other than myself, that all changed."

"Toward the end of my career I became more anxious about fires in the middle of the night, especially in commercial buildings. They just had the chance to get a lot worse before anyone noticed them. When you're coming down the block and you can't tell what building is on fire because there's so much smoke, that is creepy."

Brenda remembered another night tour on a famous date—New Year's Eve, 1999. "There was a tremendous amount of anxiety nationwide about the coming of the millennium, known at the time as Y2K. There were all these rumors, especially in New York, that there might be bombings, or a computer virus would make everything go haywire, or something would happen at Times Square. It just went on and on."

"So the fire department decided to do preplanning for Y2K. Mainly that consisted of putting big emergency generators at key firehouses, and they assigned extra people to work that night. These were brand new firefighters who were there to staff an emergency call system. The idea was that when all hell broke loose, they would be the ones to do individual dispatch and things like that."

"I was working New Year's Eve, and my firehouse was close to Times Square. We were close to all the big target areas—the Empire State Building and Penn Station and so on. I heard that we were going to have all these new kids in our firehouse, and we were going to have extra people for the meal. The officer supervising them was the most hyper and nervous person you could imagine being assigned to a role like that."

"So I decided I was going to try to take the edge off, and I went out and bought all kinds of party hats and noisemakers and brought them to the firehouse. And it turned out to be a big joke, because absolutely nothing happened that night. Even the normal craziness you would get from being around Times Square didn't happen. We were expecting to be really busy, but I don't know that we turned a wheel that night. We basically spent the entire night just marching around in our party hats and blowing our noisemakers and taking photos of ourselves acting really goofy. It turned out to be an enormous joke on the city because all this money had been spent and all these preparations made, and it turned out to be a total bust."

Brenda's early career was marked by obstacles related to her role in getting women hired on the FDNY, but even in the hard times, she never lost her love and sense of purpose for the job. "I would like to be remembered as a person who really wanted to help other people in many different ways. I wanted to help boys and girls pursue their passion regardless of gender. I'd like to be remembered for making the fire service better, for making it more professional and safer."

"One of the most gratifying things for me is to have been a role model for little girls. When I was growing up, there weren't that many role models for girls other than being a mother, homemaker, maybe a teacher or secretary or nurse. Other than that, in my childhood, there weren't other possibilities for girls. I've been really blessed in my career. I've had the chance to travel the world, meet interesting people, and try to make a difference with my life. Not a lot of people get that opportunity."

Augusta Turner at the South Central Regional meeting of the International Association of Black Professional Fire Fighters

Augusta Turner

# Sleepwear

Augusta Turner was the first woman hired with the Monroe, Louisiana Fire Department in 1985. For her entire career, she remained the only woman on the department until she left in 2002. "I promised to stay until we got another female firefighter, which took nearly seventeen years. Still, in 2011, the department only has two women." Before becoming a firefighter, Augusta was going to school to become a cosmetologist. Since leaving the department, Augusta has run a home health care business and a radio station.

Augusta was not welcomed on the job as the first woman, and one night she had some unexpected visitors at the fire station. "I remember when I was first hired, there were no partitions or anything in the dormitories where we all slept at night. At this one station, we had watch duty, and the least senior person had the watch at night when the guys were sleeping, from midnight until four in the morning. So this was my watch, and one night, the guys' wives decided to come to the station around one in the morning, because they knew their husbands would be sleeping."

The women confronted Augusta, asking her why she had wanted to become a firefighter, and where she slept in the fire station. "I said I sleep in a room, in a bed. And they said, who do you sleep in the room with? And I said, with the driver. And this woman said, you sleep in the room with my husband? I said, well, if he's the driver at the time, I sleep in the room with your husband."

"And she said, well what do you wear? I said I usually wear jogging pants. But that's not the question. The question is, what does your husband wear? Your husband wears a tee shirt and his underpants. Sometimes, they don't wear no tee shirt, no socks, no nothing. And the wives got very agitated. I told them, I wear my jogging pants. I don't wear no pajamas or lingerie or anything. I wear jogging pants, but your husband wears his boxers, and no tee shirt, no socks. They say that's tradition, what they've done all the time, and I'm not trying to get them to change for me. But the minute they start touching me or making remarks, you will hear about it."

"From that point on, the men started wearing jogging pants and tee shirts to bed, stuff that was appropriate for having a woman in the room. I had the wives start taking up for me. They said, well, that's not fair. Word started getting out. Do you know how your husband is sleeping in the room with this woman? You wouldn't want your daughter to sleep in a room with a man like that. You wouldn't want to do that. So the women started being advocates for me. I was able to turn a negative into a positive."

"Later they moved me to a place called Sellman Field. It was known as The Rock. Nobody wanted to go there. They'd break you. My mindset was just getting my job done and going home. I had no time for stupidity. Being the first, I had to endure a lot of things and be smart about how I did it."

"These guys were old military guys and were not going to change for me no matter what. They were sleeping with no clothes on. They said that's the way they slept at home and that's the way they were going to sleep there. So I decided to bring my camera to work. When the alarm went off in the middle of the night, the lights came on, and I started snapping the pictures. Men with no clothes on, with no tee shirt, with just boxers. I snapped it all."

"When we were out on the run, everyone wanted the camera. But I gave the camera to someone I knew at the fire and told him I'd get it from him the next day. So I didn't even have it when the guys asked for it, and they searched my locker up and down trying to find it. The next day I went and made copies of the film and showed it to them the next shift. And I told them, every one of these pictures will be in the paper because there is a thing you call respect. And you wouldn't want someone from your family to be subjected to what I'm going through. I had no more problems out of them after that."

"They learned to respect me. But they called me a troublemaker too. So I started doing my research. I looked in Ebony Magazine, and I saw this woman firefighter named Pat Dyas in Shreveport. So I called Shreveport, and I said, I want to talk to this woman. Could you please give her my number? She called me back in an hour. And I said, I need to know about this black firefighters association because I'm having hell being the first female. Pat got in her van and came to Monroe the next day. And she coached me through. Hold your head up, she said. Don't quit. Things are going to get better. It's going to be tough, but hang in there. And I joined the black firefighters organization the next day." Augusta ultimately started a local chapter of the International Association of Black Professional Fire Fighters in Monroe.

"My purpose in starting the organization was for other females to get educated on becoming firefighters, and for black firefighters to develop skills to become a driver or a captain or a chief. I wanted the community to know that as black firefighters, we do more than just fight fire. We help our communities. I want more women in the fire service. Once women are given the opportunity, we're great at what we do. Just give us an equal chance."

Jen Collins-Brown at a funeral for a Salem, MA firefighter who died in the line of duty

Jen Collins-Brown

# The Ink Plant Explosion

Jen Collins-Brown is a fire captain and paramedic with the Topsfield, Massachusetts Fire Department. Topsfield, a residential community around 25 miles northeast of Boston, has a combination department that includes both full time and paid-on-call firefighters. Jen was an on-call firefighter for over eighteen years before becoming full time in 2006. Before becoming a full time firefighter, Jen worked as an occupational therapist and is the mother of four children. Her oldest son recently joined her department as an on-call firefighter.

One of Jen's most memorable calls occurred in the middle of the night in 2006. "An ink plant had exploded in the town of Danvers,

next to Topsfield. It was the day before Thanksgiving in the very
early morning. I could feel the explosion at my home. I got up and
my husband said, where are you going? And I said, I don't know, but
I'm going somewhere, I know that."

"When we arrived and presented ourselves to command, we were told
to search the buildings that remained standing. They were mostly
single family or two or three family structures. We searched for a
couple hours through each building. What was amazing to me, and
what really stuck with me, was that these were people who were in
their beds asleep—it was two or three in the morning when the
explosion occurred—and we were going through their houses and
seeing their beds exploded into other rooms."

"I was imagining what it must be like to find your children and other
family members when the stairs weren't where they were supposed to
be, and nothing looked the same. There was no electricity. There
were places we went into and the faucet was on, like someone was
getting a drink, and then suddenly their lives were blown apart by this
explosion."

"I marveled at the unbelievable courage and strength of these people
to get out of those buildings. Because almost no one got hurt; there
were only minor injuries among the people in the houses. It was
remarkable because the explosion was felt many miles away, as far
away as New Hampshire. The damage to the buildings in that three
or four block area was extensive. One of the buildings involved was
the New England Home for the Deaf. The staff there did such an
amazing job getting those residents out."

"I was so affected by the fact I was in someone's home, thinking
about where they were sleeping, and suddenly it was all gone. Those
people had to pull themselves out of a sleep and find their loved ones
in the dark in a building that didn't resemble anything like what it did
just a minute before. Walking through their homes, we'd see their
possessions, dishes and fish tanks and everything they owned, and
everything was exploded and completely wrecked. The scope of the

destruction was unimaginable, but the people were so strong. If that had been me, I don't know if I could have done as well. There was a tremendous volume of fire at the scene, because of all the chemicals at the printing plant. And yet no one was killed; they were all able to get themselves out."

Working on a combination department with only a few career members brings particular challenges. As a full time firefighter, Jen works with only one other person. "We have to work extra hard to make sure the full time and call firefighters work well together, and that everyone feels comfortable with everyone else's training. Having been a call firefighter for eighteen years I can say it is a very difficult position to be in, because you are expected to know everything that the full time firefighter knows, and it's not your full time job."

At night, the three full time officers rotate taking the fire truck home with them. The duty officer then responds with the truck and the on-call firefighters respond to the scene. "Because we're coming from home at night, we all usually have our pajamas on under our turnout gear. So we compare pajamas. I have these pink fuzzy pajamas with frogs on them."

"I'm proud to show my girls they can do this job if they choose to. My role model has been my mother, who is a very strong woman and is amazing in the things she has done. She got her pilot's license when her five kids went to college. We were looking at schools all over New England and she decided the only way she could keep in touch with all of us was to get her pilot's license." Jen laughed. "I think she secretly wanted to do it anyway. I take my lead from her."

Michelle Symes

Michelle Symes by the "Charlie MacPherson" pumper

# The Coldest Fire

Michelle Symes has been a firefighter with the Ross Ferry Volunteer Fire Department since 2008. Ross Ferry serves a community of three thousand people on Boularderie Island in Nova Scotia, an island within the larger island of Cape Breton. The Ross Ferry response district has only one fire hydrant. Michelle is the department's training officer and also a full time mother of three children. Her husband is a marine engineer who is often at sea for weeks at a time. The Ross Ferry Fire Department includes eighteen women among its thirty-six members.

Michelle remembered one of the first fires she responded to. "It was a fire in an old farmhouse down the road from me. It was in January and it was the coldest night of the entire year, around minus forty degrees. The house was a couple hundred meters from the road uphill, and the driveway had not been plowed yet for the winter. There was nearly four feet of snow in the driveway. The man had gotten out of the house but had returned several times to search for his dog. Eventually he walked with no shoes on in the snow to a neighbor's house, around half a kilometer away, and reported the fire."

"When we got there, the house was fully engulfed and there wasn't much to save. We had to carry all the equipment—the hose lines, the generators, the lights—all the way up this driveway. It took hours to get this fire out. We called for mutual aid for a water shuttle. And for some reason our radios weren't working, so if we needed more equipment or different things, or somebody else to help us, we had to trek all the way back down the driveway to pass the message on."

"The gear I had at the time had belonged to a former member of the department. The boots were size nine men's. I now have a women's six and a half that fit perfectly. My turnout gear was meant for a man about six feet tall. I am five foot two. Every step I took in those boots caused them to stick in the snow and I had to maneuver just so my foot wouldn't come out of my boots. I caught on quickly after the first few steps. My turnout coat had an elastic belt inside that snapped together at my hips, which meant when I raised my leg, it would only go up so high before it was stopped by the inside belt, making climbing uphill very difficult. Everything was ice, and you froze instantly to anything you contacted."

"After fighting the fire all night, my husband and I got home, and took turns eating and showering. I showered in the hottest water I could stand to try to thaw out. Our bunker gear was so wet and we were so cold! We had about an hour before we had to get up and help our three children get ready for school. I can remember being so cold in bed that it was hard to fall asleep. I did fall asleep, but it felt like only minutes before the morning alarm went off. My hair was still wet from the shower. I was literally chilled for two days after that fire."

"I can remember thinking, what am I doing? I'm a stay-at-home mom; I have no business being a firefighter. But sometimes your heart tells your head what you're meant to do, and I think that's what happened to me. In my heart, I am a firefighter."

# Chapter 10

## The Future of Women in Firefighting

On September 10, 2001, women firefighters were doing pretty well. At that point, women had been career firefighters in the United States for over 25 years, and had served as volunteers for much longer than that. Although still a distinct minority, the numbers of women who chose firefighting as a career or vocation were steadily rising. Many women had promoted to officer, battalion chief, or other leadership positions. Some had even become chief of their departments. Gear had improved and safety equipment was readily available in every size. Many departments had made at least an initial effort to modify facilities to better accommodate women. The ubiquitous label of "fireman" for anyone engaged in firefighting was even giving way to the more inclusive and technically correct "firefighter."

Then came 9/11. That terrible day changed many things, on both a global and personal scale. For the thousands of people who lost family members and friends that day, life would never be the same. The New York City Fire Department lost 343 members that day, a loss that would have been unimaginable just the day before, and which changed the history and culture of that organization forever.

The terrible events of September 11, 2001 began an era of change for women firefighters. Suddenly it was not only okay but also somehow preferred to start using the term "fireman" again. Many fire departments adopted a back-to-basics philosophy, not only in skills training but also in hiring and promotion. Things like recruitment among diverse populations took a back seat to terrorism preparedness. Women were still firefighters, officers, and chiefs, but were much less visible than they had been just the year before. The idea of a gender-integrated fire service did not have the traction it had even months earlier. Women were still being hired as firefighters, but often in smaller numbers. Some fire departments, including my own, did not hire a single woman as a firefighter in the ten years after 9/11.

What is the future for women in the fire service? Experienced women firefighters are getting older, and younger women may or may not be taking their places. For new women entering the fire service, the working conditions they find will be quite different from what women encountered in the 1970s and 1980s. For the most part, the fire service of 2011 is more professional, more skilled, and better equipped than it was thirty years earlier. Firefighters have more responsibilities today than they did in the past, but they also have better training, better equipment, and in many cases, better leadership.

There is an emphasis today on health and wellness in the fire service. Lifelong fitness is a challenge for women the same as it is for men. "I never really thought about being a woman doing this job," said Margaret Meisner of the Ivyland Fire Company in Bucks County, Pennsylvania. "But I do think about being an older, more mature person doing it, since I am now in my forties. I can keep up with the young kids. I can haul that ladder. I can hook up the hydrant. I have shown my son that I can do anything I put my mind to. I want him to judge people not by age or gender, but for who they are and what they contribute." Meg Richardson of the Marietta, Georgia Fire Department echoed that sentiment. "I will strive over the remaining nine years of my career to maintain and set the example of fitness for duty."

Women who join the fire service must be prepared for personal changes as well as physical challenges. "It's affected my entire life," said Jen Reeser of the Avon, Connecticut Fire Department. "When I joined, I was very young, and was quiet, shy and would get embarrassed easily. I can still be quiet, but my shyness is gone. And it takes a lot to get me embarrassed." On a wider scale, "this job has opened my eyes," said Nancy Repetto of the Wagontown, Pennsylvania Fire Department. "I almost felt I had tunnel vision before. After becoming a firefighter, I began to see how many people there were who needed help. Being a firefighter has made me less selfish. I have developed more of a concern for others' well-being. And I think being a firefighter has also made me a better parent."

For women firefighters, it is not enough to simply survive in the long haul. They must find ways to use their unique gifts and abilities to allow not only their organizations to thrive, but also themselves personally. A positive attitude in the face of adversity certainly helps. "There was opposition," said Annie Thelen of the Mt. Calvary, Wisconsin Fire Department. "But I choose not to look at it that way. We're just here to help. That's all."

Commitment is a critical component of a full fire service career. Success for Marlene Juttens of the Chatham-Kent, Ontario Fire Department was all about "hard work and perseverance. I hope the newer women don't have to go through what I did. Maybe one of them might become chief. Things are different now." Kim Hood of the Fairfax County, Virginia Fire Department spoke of personal values that have served her as an officer. "My crew knows I will fight for them. I don't stand back. I am part of the group. They see me participating. They know that I expect every patient to be treated fairly and equally, even the drunk at two in the morning that you've already run on three times this month."

Setting personal boundaries and being willing to act on them are important strategies for success as a woman firefighter. "I've been very fortunate with the guys I have worked with," said Jenny Oltmann of the Eastside, Washington Fire-Rescue Department. "I run into a couple guys who are chauvinistic, but I just let them know, I don't have time for your garbage. I'm not here for that. I'm here because I passed the test like everybody else. I just want to do a job. And I do it well." When working with people who might try to test her limits, Jenny said, "I let them know, here's the boundary. You get one warning. I had one guy step over that boundary, and I said, all right, I'm going to write you up. I'm not putting up with this. As result, that person was formally reprimanded, and the other guys all said to me, hey, way to go. Way to stand up for yourself."

Longevity as a firefighter depends on taking care of yourself, physically, psychologically, and emotionally. "This job shows you what can happen if you don't take care of yourself," said Rebecca Kelly of the Fairfax County, Virginia Fire Department. "I try to notice if someone I've known for awhile just isn't acting right. I've taken the time in my career to become an EEO counselor and to do mediation. I want to help people deal with things that may be bothering them." Rebecca also commented on the need to give that attention to herself. "My husband (who is also a firefighter) and I have made a commitment to do something for our marriage every year. The incidence of divorce is high in this career. We made a commitment to each other to further our relationship and communication. That's the number one thing you'll hear not only as a problem on the fire ground but also in relationships— communication."

The skills and abilities needed to be a successful firefighter are varied and challenging. One must be not only physically strong, but also healthy and fit. Technical and mechanical skills are necessary to operate the equipment and troubleshoot the inevitable breakdowns. Interpersonal and communication skills are critical not only for successfully interacting with the diverse service community, but especially for forming effective teams with other emergency responders. Firefighters need to have a generalist approach to knowledge and a desire to never stop learning.

In many ways, women in 2011 are better equipped to meet the challenges of firefighting than they were in 1980. Girls have more access to elite sports programs and there is more positive reinforcement for participation than there was thirty years ago. Physical fitness is a national value in 2011, not just a personal one. Young women have equal opportunities to pursue college degrees in fire science and related fields that make them more competitive as firefighter candidates. Women today have an expectation that any field of work they want to engage in will be open to them.

Why then do many fire departments report that they have trouble getting women to take the hiring test? Why is attrition still a problem among women firefighters? With the clear commitment that is demonstrated by women on the job, why do some fire agencies conclude that women just aren't interested in becoming firefighters anymore?

One key issue for the future of women firefighters is visibility. With women representing less than 5% of the total firefighters in the United States, and even fewer in other countries, most people have probably never seen a woman firefighter. It is hard to imagine yourself doing a job if you have never seen anyone who looks like you in that job.

This is the real value of recruitment programs, not only for women but for all underrepresented groups in the fire service. Recruitment is not about talking someone into a job that he or she might not really want, but rather making that job seem possible, and allowing the individual to make an informed decision about pursuing it or not. It is hard enough just being a firefighter, but few individuals want to also take on the role of pioneer, ground breaker, and representative of an entire gender as well. Women just want to do the job, the same as men.

Programs like summer fire camps for girls are a big step in the right direction. In these programs, young women not only get hands-on experience with firefighting but also learn from women in positions of expertise and leadership. They see women doing the job of firefighter and say to themselves: Well, maybe I could do that too.

Cadet and internship programs are another way to bring women into the fire service. Structured programs that allow real world experience along with mentoring and training can allow young women and men to gain skills and confidence and compete for jobs at a much higher level. College and technical programs that provide a combination of academics and practical experience also provide accessibility to careers and vocations perhaps not previously considered.

On the good days, being a firefighter is the best job in the world. It is certainly a job or vocation that may provide challenge and satisfaction to women equally as it does for men, but women often do not have equal opportunity to experience these rewards. "This job truly opened my eyes to the reality that there is still a lot of inequality out there for men and women," said Jeanne Pashalek, a battalion chief with the Lincoln, Nebraska Fire Department. "In 2011, you wouldn't think we'd have this much work to do. But having been through it personally, and hearing numerous testimonies from other individuals, I know there is a big gap out there that we have to close. I'm proud that as a woman I have proved I can do the job. Women are certainly capable of doing the job given the opportunity to do so. I want to leave a legacy to pave the way for other women. If I can make their path to success any easier by what I've gone through, then it is all worth it to me."

In 2011, some women don't care if they are referred to as "firemen." Indeed, some women use this term to describe themselves. For many others, it is long past time when the more accurate "firefighter" should be the norm. But language is only a small part of the picture. For the fire service to be truly inclusive and to best represent and serve its communities, it is critical that women and men are equally included and recognized for the work they do and the sacrifices they make. It is not just a brotherhood anymore.

# Photo Credits
(in order of appearance in book)

Cover- Annie Webb- photo courtesy of Gwen Harp
Historic women firefighters—Photo courtesy of Women in the Fire Service, Inc.
Dee Wooley—Photo courtesy of Dee Wooley
Katja Lancing—Photo courtesy of Richard Lancing
Michele Fitzsimmons—Photo courtesy of Joelle Gozlan
Brita Horn—Photo courtesy of Steve Smyres and Jim Bradford
Sandy Schiess—Photo courtesy of Alan L. Davison
Komako Goolsby—Photo courtesy of Komako L. Goolsby
Anna Schermerhorn-Collins—Photo courtesy of Diana DiPrima
Debra Addison—Photo courtesy of Rahman D. Addison
Cheryl Clark—Photo courtesy of Merritt Colton
Amy Brow—Photo courtesy of Carol Lentz
Mary Cooper—Photo courtesy of Mary M. Cooper
Christine Bahr—Photo courtesy of Christine Bahr
Denise Allen—Photo courtesy of Courtney Looke
Shelia Vitalis—Photo courtesy of Shelia Vitalis
Chassity Pollard—Photo courtesy of David J. Summers
Maria Figueroa—Photo courtesy of Maria Figueroa
Annie Webb—Photo courtesy of Gwen R. Harp
Meg Richardson—Photo courtesy of Johnny Walker
Carol Murphy—Photo courtesy of Rick White
Susan Salinger—Photo courtesy of Craig Allyn Rose
Sarah Twomey—Photo courtesy of Sarah Twomey
Karrie Leigh Boswell—Photo courtesy of the International Association of Fire Fighters
Katherine Ridenhour—Photo courtesy of Paul Dillon
Patricia Dyas—Photo courtesy of Chris Henry, Custom Shots Photography LLC
Tamala Wilson—Photo courtesy of Lennis Harris
Nicol Juratovac—Photo courtesy of Rigel Juratovac
Krista Wyatt—Photo courtesy of Krista Wyatt
Karen Simpson—Photo courtesy of Karen Simpson
Beth Heim—Photo courtesy of Chris A. Skelly
Lynette Jelinek—Photo courtesy of Lynette Jelinek
Joette Borzik—Photo courtesy of Joette Borzik
Brenda Berkman—Photo courtesy of Brenda Berkman
Augusta Turner—Photo courtesy of Pat Dyas
Jen Collins-Brown—Photo courtesy of Jen Collins-Brown
Michelle Symes—Photo courtesy of W. Dwayne Symes

# Acknowledgements

First and foremost, I wish to thank Brian Bahr for his generous offer of help to a stranger to make this book happen. I could not have done it without him.

Thank you to Christine Bahr for her support and encouragement throughout the project.

I am grateful to my family: Nick, Joey, Adam, and Adrian, for their support for this project, and for women firefighters generally.

Thank you to Terry Floren for her many years of work to support women firefighters and especially her work in preserving the early history.

Finally and most especially, I wish to thank all the women who serve their communities as firefighters and emergency responders, only a few of whom are represented here. You make a difference every day.

CPSIA information can be obtained at www.ICGtesting.com
Printed in the USA
BVOW012207031212

307205BV00007B/96/P